Friends @ lake cities —
Thank
widows
a safe place
May the Lord bless your
ministry & encourage
the widowed in your
congregation.

[signature]

widowed

ENDORSEMENTS

"Nearly 700,000 women lose their husbands each year, and they will be widows for an average of fourteen years. Fran Geiger Joslin, who knows the rough seas of such grief, writes as an empathic companion. As one who has 'been there,' she explores a broad range of questions such as What should I put on the headstone? What do I do with my desire for physical intimacy? And Shouldn't I feel better by now? Drawing from her journals, experiences, and research, Joslin has created in *Widowed: When Death Sucks the Life out of You* a work that takes readers into the uncharted waters of 'the new normal' and helps them find calmer seas."

Sandra Glahn, PhD, Author
Associate Professor of Media Arts and Worship
Editor-in-chief of *Kindred Spirit*

"I wish my widowed friends had this book when they experienced the heartbreak of losing a spouse. Full of practical, empathetic information, Joslin's book serves as a needed friend on an unwanted but necessary journey after grief. I highly recommend this book."

Mary DeMuth
Speaker and author of more than thirty books including,
The Day I Met Jesus

"Fran Geiger Joslin has tackled a tough topic with grace and wisdom. The death of a spouse can plunge us unwillingly into an abyss of despair. If our sorrows remain unattended, those of us left behind will wither and die with our loved ones. Fran's book offers hope and healing to those who dare to tackle the darkness head on."

Rita A. Schulte, LPC; Widow; Author of
Shattered: Finding Hope and Healing through the Losses of Life,
Imposter: Gain Confidence, Eradicate Shame and Become Who God Made You to Be

"*Widowed: When Death Sucks the Life out of You* is a frank discussion regarding the hard and painful experiences of a widow in a culture that doesn't have a good appreciation for how to respond to grief and suffering. Fran Geiger Joslin takes you behind the curtain of her painful journey through the grief of widowhood, answering the questions you never before thought to ask, shedding light on the concerns no one ever wants to have to face, and validating the many emotions a widow might reasonably be expected to experience. Throughout her candid discussion and recollection of her own experience, Fran also reveals God's faithfulness through the pain. *Widowed* is a valuable resource for anyone who has recently become widowed, for those who anticipate that journey in the near future, or for the friends and family who love them."

Dr. Michelle Bengtson

Author, speaker,

Board certified clinical neuropsychologist

"Having personally walked with Fran through her heart wrenching journey of grief, it is a testimony to God's redeeming work in her life that her suffering and vulnerability can now provide encouragement to other widows. She normalizes numerous aspects of the grief process and provides practical tips for those struggling to adapt to life without their loved one. While recognizing spiritual struggles often accompany the loss of a spouse, Fran unashamedly turns her readers to the ultimate hope, strength, and comfort which she herself has found in a relationship with Christ and in his Word. Though the book is written primarily for widows, friends and family will also benefit from learning what is helpful and what is not, as they seek to minister to the grieving."

Beth Gregory

Pastoral Counseling Associate, Calvary Church

Lancaster, PA

"I really appreciated realizing others have the same problems I experience. *Widowed* helped me to know that what I'm going through is completely normal. Even after being widowed a year, I find it gets harder. People in my life haven't forgotten my loss. I think they just don't know how much even a phone call, a hug—or other bit of help—can make such a difference to a widow and her family. Reading *Widowed* helped me to understand others in the same or similar situations, and I know it will help others to do the same."

Ellen, Widow

WIDOWED

WHEN DEATH SUCKS THE LIFE OUT OF YOU

FRAN GEIGER JOSLIN

AUTHENTICITY
BOOK HOUSE

10 9 8 7 6 5 4 3 2 1
Published by Authenticity Book House
Printed in the United States of America

Authenticity Book House
c/o Proven Way Ministries
The Hope Center
2001 W. Plano Parkway, Suite 3422
Plano, TX 75075 USA

DEDICATION

To my Brian: Your illness was a very long and hard road, but your loving-kindness, lack of complaint, and perfectly timed humor made the path easier. You constantly reminded me that "We're gonna make it, Babe," because "God is *good*; a *refuge* in the time of trouble. He *cares* for those who put their trust in him (Nahum 1:7)."

Through the nine-year journey, I often wondered who would support, challenge, and encourage me when you were gone. Once again, you were right. God *is* good. He *is* a refuge in times of trouble. He *does* care for those who put their trust in him.

And, by God's grace, I am making it, Babe.

ACKNOWLEDGEMENTS

The words "Thank you" don't begin to express the heartfelt gratitude I feel now that publication is within sight.

Thank you, my heavenly Father, for giving me the strength to endure a nine-year battle with cancer, the loneliness of widowhood, and the terrifying yet exhilarating experience of putting a book together.

Thank you Mom, Beth, Alice, Leah, Susan, Kris, Jenny, Denise, LuAnn, Carol, Shelley, Barbara, Cindy, Carolyn, Dorothy, and so many more who listened and prayed me through.

Thank you Howard, Paul, Steffi, Drew, Chad, Jessica, Hannah, AJ, Matt, and Nikki for supporting me through this journey of becoming a published author.

Thank you Don, Alice, Donald, Sharon, Sarah, Joe, Margaret, Jason, and kids for allowing me the privilege of being a part of Brian's family.

Thank you Mary, Leslie, D'Ann, Sandi, and Trisha for teaching me better writing skills, holding me accountable to good writing, encouraging me along the way, and for sharing your own words, which helped bring this book to life.

Thank you, Ashley Scarbrough (WrittenShutter.com) for the front cover picture which re-creates the emotional moment every widow experiences when circling the word "widowed" for the first time. It takes our breath away.

CONTENTS

PART III. When Death no Longer Wins

INTRODUCTION

I found myself terribly unprepared for widowhood—even though my husband's terminal diagnosis gave me almost nine years to plan. Few people spoke to me about widowhood, and yet I knew lots of widows. I wondered why they stay silent.

I think widows become conditioned to shut up. Our friends advise us to "move on" or "get over it." Our response? We stop talking. We tuck our feelings away in a closet. We hide our tears behind closed doors and pretend everything's okay.

I hereby declare a moratorium on silence. I will not stay silent. Dwelling in silence helps no one. In fact, it perpetuates fear, indecision, and the entire grief process. We must talk about the pain in order to help others who face this terrible disease called "widowhood."

Do you feel all alone?

Do you wonder if you will make it?

Do you feel no one wants to listen or seems to care that you've practically lost your mind in the throes of grief?

I wrote *Widowed: When Death Sucks the Life out of You* because I couldn't find the book I needed on the shelves at the bookstore. I couldn't find even one book that addressed the specific needs I experienced as a widow. Yes, I found a chapter or two here and there, but not one author talked about the realities I faced on a daily basis.

I hope by reading this book you will find relief instead of pain. I hope you will find peace and camaraderie instead of isolation and aloneness. Allow yourself the luxury of crying your way through it, if that's what it takes.

Normal, normal, normal! If you get nothing else from this book, I want you to understand that your feelings qualify as completely normal. Widowhood exists as a unique form of loss. According to WidowsHope.org, widowhood ranks number one among stressors. In the United States, 800,000 people (700,000 of whom are female) find themselves widowed every year. Worldwide, 245 million end up widowed, and of those, 115 million live in poverty.[1]

Grief literally sucks the life out of us widows, who are left to fend for ourselves. We feel alone in our pain and afraid to tell the truth because people around us can't seem to handle it. Even well-meaning friends often inquire as to how we are doing, yet they don't stick around long enough to hear the answer.

I wrote *Widowed: When Death Sucks the Life out of You* to encourage other widows and to address the concerns I suffered as a widow but to which I found no answers. I purposely wrote it in short sections because those who grieve find it difficult to focus.

Because I want you to quickly find answers to your needs and questions, similar stories or bits of advice are sometimes intentionally found in more than one section.

All of the stories I tell are true, but to protect identities, other than immediate family members, names within the book are fictitious. I often refer to widows as a general term including both widows and widowers.

I write from a faith-based perspective. My faith kept my head above water and anchored my soul through the agony and loneliness of widowhood.

I write to tell widows what to expect because no one told me. Nor did they offer advice or comfort. My goal? To change that. To give you some tools for this long and lonely road. Things they don't tell us:

- The torture and misery of loneliness.
- What it's like to wrestle with our thoughts, feelings, lack of sleep, or too much sleep.
- How we feel like our legs can't move, not sure we can go on one more day.
- The depth of the raw emotion.
- The number of hours each day spent crying.
- How our brains get so foggy.
- How to deal with all of the "well-wishers" who want to rush us into remarriage.
- How to deal with inappropriate suitors.
- How to deal with the opposite sex, new or conflicting feelings and attraction, but still not ready or able to date.
- That we don't actually cry *all* of the time. It is such a reprieve to laugh!

- That the second year was as bad as—or worse than—the first year.

- What it's like to desire a companion but be unable to commit to any relationship other than a friendship.

- How to deal with depression.

- The issue—or lack—of sex.

MY STORY

I married my first love—Brian Geiger—on April 8, 1989. The most amazing day of my life! I couldn't imagine anything better. Or happier. As I approached the church to dress for the wedding, I saw him standing in the courtyard. God smiled on me, and this day it was my turn to say, "I do." I ran and jumped into his arms. "I get to spend the rest of my life with this man," I thought.

Ten years and three children later, everything changed. October 14, 1999. "It is a very impressive mass," the nurse foolishly jested. My world came to a screeching halt. Suddenly brain surgery, chemotherapy, and radiation permeated our everyday lives. Doctor's appointments became constant, and trips to the cancer center in Houston offered the only opportunity for dates. I learned to converse intelligently about brain cancer. My mind grasped more information than I ever thought possible and certainly more than I ever wanted to know.

We lived moment to moment, month to month, year to year, always praying for a miracle. Survival mode dictated daily life, and I wondered how on earth my kids would survive our new chaotic life. By God's grace we persevered, though I must say at times I didn't think I would make it.

I found myself living in two worlds, yet I managed to stay organized in only one. I couldn't keep up with the teachers' requests for signed paperwork. I couldn't keep track of kids and their homework. The laundry got washed, but I struggled to put it away, much less iron it. My house? Well, you can imagine.

I lost Brian piece by piece over a period of almost nine years and grieved every loss. He kept his sense of humor though, which gave me strength to keep going. I wondered how I would cope once he went to heaven and could no longer bring laughter to our home.

Brian wasn't one to consider death. His plan embraced life, with the goal of one day walking his seven-year-old daughter down the aisle on her wedding day. April 8, 2004. We celebrated our 15th anniversary enjoying dinner out, paid for by a loving, generous lady from our church. Then he took me to the jewelry store. We had no money, but he splurged anyway. "Just in case I don't make it to our twenty year anniversary," he told me. How thoughtful and generous. I still wear that beautiful ring.

April 8, 2008. Our 19th anniversary. Brian's cancer no longer responded to treatment. Though we flew to Houston twice a month for $20,000 infusion chemo treatments, we were weary and losing hope. By this time I asked the Lord to give me twenty years with Brian. Just one more year.

Our marriage ended at nineteen. Brian met the Lord in July, and so began the rest of my life *without* him.

To explain the loss of your other half? Impossible! Many describe it as the amputation of a limb. Half of you really. The logical one. The funny one. The easygoing one. The one who complements your very being. The one who knows you better than anyone else in the world. The one who comforts you in your hour of greatest need. Ironic, since this hour of need exists primarily because he was ripped from your life here on earth and can no longer serve as the comfort you so desperately crave.

In the interest of full disclosure, God graciously gifted me with another wonderful, funny, and remarkable man, a widower himself. Howard Joslin also perfectly complements my personality, and I love life with him. I experience great joy and happiness with Howard, but I also still miss Brian. Yes, I remarried, but I will always remain Brian Geiger's widow.

I still feel the pain of loss. Certain dates and holidays still shut me down emotionally. I often still cry when a new friend tells me she's a widow. My heart grieves for the widowed because a spouse's death sucks the life out of us.

Part One

WHEN DEATH STRIKES

SHOCK

"There's a fine edge to new grief, it severs nerves, disconnects reality—there's mercy in a sharp blade. Only with time, as the edge wears, does the real ache begin."

~Christopher Moore

Shock hits almost immediately following the trauma of losing a loved one. Meriam-Webster.com defines shock as "a disturbance in the equilibrium or permanence of something: a sudden or violent mental or emotional disturbance."[1] I can identify with the word *violent*. Brian's death violently ripped him from my life.

Shock-Absorbing Grace

Have you ever wondered why sometimes the well-wishers at the visitation and funeral seem to be in worse shape emotionally than the family? Oddly, the protection of shock doesn't seem to cover everyone. For the most part, the average friend, colleague, or acquaintance continues to miss the deceased, but his life goes on fairly normally, interrupted only here and there by the loss. Initially, shock seems to absorb the worst of the pain for those closest to the deceased whose death destroys their daily existence.

I knew lots of people would attend Brian's funeral and viewing. He was well-known and well-liked. My body, however, went weak upon his death. I continually sucked in deep breaths, as if I couldn't get enough air. Overwhelmed by the amount of work, time, effort, and thought that goes into planning a funeral and burial, I just wanted to lie down and sleep, though sleep would not come.

I felt physically ill the night before the viewing. I feared the thought of standing and greeting so many people. I dreaded dealing with their reactions to my loss and Brian's dead body laid out beside me. A wise friend suggested I sit on a stool at the entrance to the adjoining room and form the line from there.

People began arriving early, and to my surprise I never made it to the stool. Although I remember only snippets of the ordeal, I stood for three hours greeting people as if it were a party instead of a viewing. I smiled, laughed, and hugged hundreds of people without thinking of my pain. All of this in high heels, mind you.

Immediately after the crowd left and the funeral director handed me Brian's wedding ring, I lost all strength again and collapsed into a puddle. Shock, my friend, functions as grace given to us at just the right time—God's shock-absorbing grace.

Think Shock Absorber

Not to be confused with physiological shock, which happens after an injury, emotional shock takes place immediately after a death or emotional trauma. I've come to believe two stages of this kind of shock likely exist. The initial reaction often includes a strong emotional response like crying, wailing, shouting, or even total disbelief. Typically, this emotional trauma ushers in a more prolonged state of shock that lasts for weeks or even months and can actually serve "as an emotional anesthetic during a time of unimaginable pain," according to Kenneth Haugk, author of a three-book series, *Journeying Through Grief.*[2]

Allow me to illustrate with a comparison. Think about how cars function. Though we can feel bumps in the road, shock absorbers exist to soften the blow—or how much bumpiness we actually feel. You could say God gives us a built-in shock absorber to help navigate the first weeks after the death of our loved one.

Shock may feel frustrating because our brains struggle to fully engage, but it provides a semblance of protection. It allows us the ability to "get through" all of the tasks required in the early days after our spouse's death—namely picking out a casket, making hundreds of decisions, greeting people, and simply getting through the visitation and the funeral or memorial service. Experiencing shock doesn't mean we won't cry, or that we won't feel even physically ill, but the enormous weight of grief has not yet fully settled on our shoulders.

I attended the funeral of a ten-year-old boy a number of years ago. Grieving deeply, I found myself baffled and offended by the behavior of the family. The boy's mom, dad, and sister laughed and joked as if nothing was wrong. I now understand that God gifted them with a shock absorber at this critical time.

Decision Making

Still hospitalized three weeks after surgery, a last ditch effort to give Brian a few more months of life, he quit breathing one night and ended up on life support (another story). As a love gift to his brother, who at the time was on a mission trip halfway around the world, I made the choice to continue life support another day until his brother could get back home and say good-bye.

I think Brian's dad needed to do something during the excruciating wait. He and one of Brian's sisters took an entire morning to visit funeral homes. Too exhausted to join them at that point, I gladly let them take on the task. Their research saved me time and effort and proved invaluable in helping me narrow down my options. Sometimes the whole task is too overwhelming, but others can lighten our load by participating in part of the process.

GRIEF

"Spring becomes winter, blue turns to gray, birds go silent, and the chill of sorrow settles in. Bereavement comes from the word 'reave,' 'to take away by force, plunder, rob.' Death robs you. You are bereaved because you are robbed."

~Max Lucado

"Grief becomes like quicksand which, with a soundless kind of fury clutches at the heart, squeezing from it the very essence of life and vitality."

~James Means

"Grief is the loudest silence I have ever heard."

~Angie Cartright

Everyone experiences and expresses grief differently. All grief, therefore, fits into the normal category. So, take heart. No matter where you find yourself, know this: *You are normal.*

Author, blogger, and widow, Teresa Bruce describes grief beautifully:

Grief doesn't affect mourners 24/7; it lurks 48 hours a day, 14 days per week. (Whether "the math" agrees or not, that *is* how it feels.) Grief doesn't *visit* the homes or workplaces of those who have lost; without permission it becomes an unwelcome squatter inside the cells and hearts of the bereaved. It tosses beloved furnishings out onto rainy streets while arranging its own dark goods in every corner of memory and thought.[3]

Normal Grief

Research indicates normal grief can include any or all of the following symptoms, plus many more, I'm sure:

- Nausea
- Crying
- Sighing
- Headaches
- Loss of appetite
- Difficulty sleeping
- Weakness
- Feelings of heaviness
- Aches
- Pains
- Stress-related illness
- Sadness
- Yearning
- Worry
- Fear
- Anxiety
- Frustration
- Anger
- Guilt
- Isolation from others
- Detachment
- Questions of why, the purpose of life, the meaning of death
- Depression
- Suicidal thoughts and actions
- Post-traumatic stress syndrome.[4]

What an overwhelming list! That explains why we feel like such a mess. The experience of grief is no small thing. Now maybe we can understand the reason grief takes time and energy—a lot of time and a lot of energy.

Avoidance

Most people do anything to avoid pain in general. The temptation to run from the process of grief follows naturally. Many throw themselves into their work or into another relationship in an effort to escape the pain. All experts agree, however, that taking time to grieve benefits us more than anything, and that big, life-changing decisions should wait for at least a year. Trying to skip grief only causes more trouble in the long run. Too many people marry quickly to avoid hurting but end up divorcing because they didn't take the necessary time to grieve the loss of their first spouse.

Keep this in mind: we all go a little—or a lot—nuts while grieving. Don't trust yourself to make wise choices in big matters.

From my experience, friends, family, and coworkers willingly give us about a year to grieve. Beyond that, "Get over it and move on." I figure we should take advantage of that year and do as much "grief work" as we possibly can. Unfortunately, we can't put a time limit on grief, and many people (myself included) find the second year more unbearable than the first.

Professor, author, and widower, Jerry Sittser, profoundly states, "I realized I would have to suffer and adjust; I could not avoid it or escape it. There is no way out but ahead, into the abyss. The loss had changed my life, setting me on a course down which I had to journey whether I wanted to or not.[5] My decision to enter the darkness . . . was the first step I took toward growth, but it was also the first step I took toward pain."[6]

Notice he made a conscious decision to "enter the darkness." He realized growth, and therefore light and healing, could not exist without first making it through the darkness. Our natural instinct drives us to choose the easiest and brightest path, but freedom from pain and debilitating sorrow requires us to charge blindly into the abyss and scratch our way toward sight.

Stages of Grief

Grief entangles like a spider web. So-called experts try to describe grief by boxing it up and putting a little bow on it. Sorry folks, but there's nothing tidy about grief. Your friends will likely offer books in an effort to "fix you," but most of the books I read only frustrated me. I couldn't fit into their pretty little box. I couldn't follow the system and then "move on."

For your awareness I will list what many call the "Stages of Grief." Please know I don't fully disagree with them. In my opinion, however, the assumption that we can process through these stages and finish grieving devalues the severity and longevity of grief.

I want to make you aware of these stages because the funeral home may even send you books on them. By all means, glean helpful information from the books, but don't think yourself abnormal if you can't fit into someone else's standard.

Five Stages of grief:[7]

- Denial
- Anger

- Bargaining

- Depression

- Acceptance

Seven Stages:[8]

- Shock and Denial

- Pain and Guilt

- Anger and Bargaining

- Depression, Reflection, and Loneliness

- The Upward Turn

- Reconstruction and Working Through

- Acceptance and Hope

Three Stages:[9]

- Disbelief

- Experiencing the Loss

- Reintegration

Clearly even the experts can't agree on categorizing grief. This doesn't surprise me. Those who personally lose a loved one tend to disagree with the typical phases, although they likely admit to experiencing at least some of them.

Most people I talk to say they certainly didn't go through them in proper order and felt frustrated and offended by those who expected them to process the assumed "stages," especially in proper order. Others say they may face one or more occurrence and revisit it later, while not necessarily feeling they experienced every stage.

The process and work of grief cannot be boxed or standardized, as most people will grieve in their own way and in their own time. Feel free to kindly teach friends about your own personal journey, whether or not you fit any of the stereotypical stages.

Personality Types

Dana Barfield, who wrote *My Friend Just Lost Her Husband*, a book on finance I highly recommend, gleans information from Dr. John Trent and suggests we grieve according to our personality type.[10] While understanding personality types and how they could affect the way we grieve might help, I don't recommend counting on them to work for everyone, either. I didn't fit perfectly into any one of the personality types, nor did my needs follow accordingly.

Normally an outgoing person who thrives on people, I withdrew in my grief. To this day I guard myself around others much more than I did before Brian died. Loss changed me. Because death affects us so profoundly, we cannot—and should not—make assumptions or presuppose any kind of expectation on how we might grieve.

Talk

Talking is a necessary element to the grief journey. Talk about your love, feelings, fears, and regrets, as well as any other pain you carry. Talking helps the healing process, though it doesn't come easily for everyone. Interestingly, Jerry Sittser noted, "Friends and colleagues marveled at how well I was doing. But inside I was a walking dead man. I exacerbated the problem by telling virtually no one about my struggle."[11]

Find safe people who will listen without judgment and share in your pain. Fellow widows usually understand since they've experienced your plight. Be careful not to overwhelm any one or two people, however. Some will tire of your sadness.

If talking to friends and acquaintances becomes frustrating or unproductive, consider finding a good counselor or a grief support group. Counselors and support groups regularly help people work through their pain. The process of finding a good counselor, though, can be cumbersome and draining, not to mention expensive.

Many large churches offer counseling as well as grief support groups. In the least, they can recommend names of good counselors. Force yourself to pick up the phone and inquire.

Weep

Crying comes easily for some, but not for others. Shedding tears naturally expresses sorrow and helps to relieve bottled up feelings of loss. It takes lots of tears on many occasions, but healthy grief allows weeping. Many say they can't shed any more tears, and that may very well happen to you.

My friend Francine won't let herself cry. She thinks she needs to hold herself together and march on. Right now she can "gut it out." Eventually, though, her pain will overflow and she will no longer be able to hide it. If you find it difficult to shed tears—because you won't allow a breakdown or because the tears refuse to come—find a time to schedule your grief. Take an evening once a week for grief. Watch a sad movie, look at your favorite pictures, or whatever helps you cry. Encouraging your tears to flow strengthens your emotional health in the long run.

A close friend asked me once how I coped and then rephrased the question, "Do you still cry every day?" What a wonderfully wise—and experienced man, a widower himself. The answer to that question tells a person a lot about your emotional state. Most of us cry daily for a period of time and then slowly the times between tears stretch out, whether we are simply "cried out" or beginning to adjust.

Friends tell me the shower works as a great place to cry. I can't hide tears, though. Mine spill out everywhere.

Weariness

Weariness could pass as a synonym for the word grief. Over and over again in my journals, I wrote, "I am so weary." Grief wore me out. I found everything overwhelming and felt just plain weary. Weary of the long days and sleepless nights, weary of single parenting and feeling alone, weary of the sadness and unending tasks, weary of answering the phone as well as questions, weary of getting up and going on, weary of responsibility, weary of carrying my own burdens as well as those of my children, weary of sleeping alone, and just plain tired of reaching out to touch Brian but not finding him there.

So terribly worn out by the end of every day, I often didn't even wash my face or brush my teeth before going to bed. It seemed more than I could bear, and no one cared whether or not I did it anyway. But every morning I somehow got up and did it all over again. For that reason alone, I began to see that God's mercies really *were* new every morning.

Post-Traumatic Stress Disorder (PTSD)

After Sally's husband died she held herself together better than most, rarely sharing her emotional ups and downs. She went into ministry and made others her focus.

She remarried ten years after her husband's death. When she and her new husband returned from their honeymoon, he decided to organize the kitchen. He removed her dishes from the cabinet and prepared to replace them with the new dishes they picked out together. Sally fell apart completely.

Unable to explain her own behavior, she asked her counselor for advice. The counselor informed Sally of her PTSD diagnosis. Unfortunately, she avoided using the term in her counseling sessions with Sally.

Widows commonly present with PTSD but never realize it. Doctors don't seem to notice or mention it. We hear of soldiers experiencing PTSD, but no one thinks to inform widows they suffer from it too.

Symptoms of PTSD fall into three categories:

- Reliving traumatic events.
- Avoidance—the desire to avoid everything related to the trauma, including avoiding interaction with others.
- Exaggerated emotions—anger, irritability, crying.[12] "Problems with trust, closeness, communication, and problem solving, which may affect the way the survivor acts with others. In turn, the way a loved one responds to him or her affects the trauma survivor."[13]

Be aware of the possibility that you could experience PTSD and watch for signs. I shied away from the phone almost exclusively. I took every opportunity to text or e-mail instead of making a phone call. I couldn't commit to small tasks or projects. I feared I couldn't come through, so I shied away from any sort of obligation. I even panicked at the thought of the kids bringing their friends over. What if I couldn't handle the interaction? When Sally explained her diagnosis to me, I recognized my own PTSD.

Treatment for PTSD usually requires intense counseling and sometimes medication.[14] Although it still raises its ugly head periodically—usually at the most inopportune times—I actually began to notice recovery once I took on a full-time job and forced myself to make phone calls, take on commitments, and other things I previously avoided.

> Because of the Lord's great love we are not consumed, for his compassions never fail. They are new every morning; great is your faithfulness.
>
> *Lamentations 3:22, 23*

ABSENT FROM THE BODY

"The presence of that absence is everywhere."

~Edna St. Vincent Millay

"I went to bed in tears the last three nights. I am exhausted emotionally and physically. What I want most is Brian's arms around me."

~Journal entry: Jan. 13, 2009

I never gave much thought to the body until I faced widowhood, but suddenly I didn't know how to function without Brian's body. I could no longer snuggle up to him at night, touch him when I needed encouragement, cry in his arms, ask for his opinions, call him on the phone, or simply receive a smile from him.

Brian's body carried those beautiful eyes that made me melt every time he looked at me. His body held his soul, spirit, and personality. He put his arms around me when I needed comfort. He gave me babies. He lit up a room with laughter. And now, the very thing that literally embodied him disappeared from my life.

Absent from the Body; Present with the Lord

In 2 Corinthians 5:8, Paul tells his readers he would rather be absent from the body and present with the Lord. What a wonderful blessing for believers who die! As Paul states, absence from this earthly body means instantly and gloriously present with the Lord.

Where does that leave the widows—those of us ripped from the presence of that body in our lives and forced to dispose of it because it no longer holds life?

Amputation

It would be unnatural not to grieve the loss of the body. It held all that we loved about our spouse—including all those qualities we didn't love so much. The absence of his body in our lives feels like more than we can bear. We were, after all, "one flesh." (Gen. 2:4).

The death of a spouse, therefore, mimics an amputation of half of us. Jerry Sittser, in his book, *A Grace Disguised*, points out that, "we recover from broken limbs, not amputations."[15] James Means, author of *A Tearful Celebration*, agrees. "There is this consummate expectation that no matter how great the loss, the sorrowful should rapidly 'get over it' and go on with life as though nothing significant happened. But real grief is something you never get over. Grief is more like an amputation than a temporary sickness."[16]

Nothing can fill the gaping hole our loved one's body should fill. People who lose a limb to amputation eventually learn to function without that limb, but their life has forever changed. Losing a spouse works the same way.

Phantom Visions

Julie called me late one night, emotionally spent. While at dinner with friends, she saw her dead husband. He stood tall and broad, talking and laughing with his friends, celebrating his new fiancée, and wearing the same clothing, all the way down to his expensive shoes. Her friends saw him too. She wanted to hug him and tell him how much she missed him, but this man bore a different name. He socialized with different friends.

What did this mean? She begged me for an answer, but I could offer none—at least nothing that made sense. What she saw might represent a simple coincidence, but God may just as well have allowed it for a reason. I guessed she would see how this experience affected her over time.

Most of us at some time or other will see someone who catches our attention and makes us think of our loved one. Our hearts stop for a moment. But when the person turns around, we clearly see he or she possesses different characteristics from our loved one. While Julie's story may seem unusual in that this stranger looked almost identical to her husband, the experience is actually more common than one might think.

I do believe in God's sovereignty. Why he allows these phantom visions of our love, I can't answer. Perhaps our psychological antennas tune in, wanting so badly to catch a glimpse of the one whom we miss terribly.

For some, these phantom visions bring comfort. For others, they dredge up memories and bring great pain. This is part of the widow's plight, and just one more thing to grieve.

Encouragement

I read Sittser's book two years after my loss and found *hope* in the challenge that "Though our bodies are broken, our thoughts confused, and our emotions troubled . . . , we *can* start to become hopeful that life *can* still be good, although never in the way it was before"[17] (emphasis mine).

HEADSTONE

"The life of the dead is set in the memory of the living."
~Marcus Tullius Cicero, Philippics

Next to making decisions about burial or cremation, the casket, and funeral plans, choosing a headstone sits high atop the list of difficult decisions we must make in the early days of widowhood. Keep in mind that sales people will eagerly sell anything. And given your emotional state, you might make purchases you'll regret or can't afford. I highly recommend getting help.

Ask for assistance in researching the options and specific cemetery requirements. In the meantime, give thought to some of the recommended considerations below. Talk these over with trusted friends or family before making final decisions.

If you've already made your decisions, please don't let guilt or remorse compound your grief.

Standard
Most often the standard and cheapest marker includes only first and last names, as well as birth and death years.

Options
The numerous choices and options can overwhelm and may include the following:

- Type of granite
- The overall style of the marker
- Double headstone or a single one
- Full name or nickname
- Full dates of birth and death, or just the years
- Scripture or other saying
- Organ donation

- Military service
- Picture

Every additional option will likely cost more money. Remember, the marker speaks to you, not your loved one. At this stage they don't care. *Do not* put yourself in a financial bind, no matter what you desire.

Purpose
First, think about the purpose of the marker.

- Is it simply marking whose body lies below?
- Do you want to consider future family history?
- Is your decision based solely on finances?
- Do you want the marker to state your beliefs or those of the deceased?
- Do you want to use scripture as a testimony to others or for your own comfort?
- Do you want to tell a simple story of your loved one (for example, to indicate organ donation, military service, loving mother, dearly beloved)?

Double vs. Single
As for the idea of a double marker, honestly consider your age, financial situation, and possible future plans or changes. A friend advised me to purchase the spot next to Brian but not to order a double marker. Young widows and widowers especially need to consider the realistic possibility of remarriage at some point, even though it feels unimaginable and undesirable at this juncture.

I chose not to order a double marker, but since then I realized most children (adult children included) prefer to bury their parents together. I remarried, but we made plans based on circumstances and our children's wishes. My new husband, Howard, purchased a double marker in his hometown of Iowa, where generations of his family lie. We will take his body back to Iowa and bury him next to his first wife. The family will bury me next to Brian in Texas.

I don't regret my decision for a single marker. Had I purchased a double marker when Brian died, my new last name would not be included. I never considered that possibility! Now I want all of my names on my marker because that's who

I am—Frances Ruth Lockhart Geiger Joslin. It will take one large stone to accommodate just my names. Heaven help us if I end up marrying a third time!

I recently read the story of an older man who removed his double marker years after his wife's death. His reasoning: "This was her grave, not mine. . . . The headstone seemed to say that I was to continue some form of a relationship with my deceased wife."[18] This may feel offensive and horrific to you. It may also seem over the top. Replacing the marker undoubtedly cost him a lot of money but, for him, the double marker represented something that stunted his ability to move forward. In the early stages of grief, you can't possibly anticipate your future responses or feelings. Give thoughtful consideration to your options, however.

Scripture

Before Brian's death, I joined my friend in visiting her husband's grave on her first birthday after his death. As we stood there, she gently recommended I put scripture on Brian's marker when the time came. I made a mental note. Though I considered it a cool idea at the time, I didn't fully "get it" until after Brian died.

I wanted to use the scripture passage that carried us through his nine-year battle with brain cancer. A well-intentioned person balked at the idea after he calculated the numbers. Every additional letter cost about two dollars more, but every extra dollar was worth it!

Nahum 1:7: "The Lord is good; a stronghold in the day of trouble. He cares for those who put their trust in him." This meaningful verse hung in large lettering over my piano but, that version—even though it says the same thing—means so much less hanging over the piano than it does when I sit weeping at the cemetery.

When we're alone and feeling weary of the pain, encouraging scripture speaks volumes and enables us to cling to the Lord while in the throes of grief. I decided, in the end, to use only the first half of the verse. For months afterward, I frequently sat on the grave and read those words, praying over them, and weeping. God *is* good even though Brian's body lies in the grave, and I experience that reminder every time I visit.

Ministry

Brian died entirely too young at forty-five years old. I wanted him to continue ministering to others in his death. At one time or another, most of us walk through a cemetery and read other markers out of curiosity. Scripture on a gravestone acts as a wonderful way to share Brian's faith in his Savior.

Family history

Depending on your financial status and whether family history matters to you, consider including all names (first, middle, last, and any other legal name), as well as exact birth and death dates. In this era of computers, all of this information exists online, which makes it more a choice than a necessity.

Organ Donation

The National Donor Organization provides an emblem for free if your spouse was an organ donor. Ask about this at the funeral home.

U.S. Military

The military provides free burial and a basic marker in their own cemeteries. Should you choose to use another cemetery, you can still include military information.

DENIAL

"If you cut your finger, you bleed. If you lost someone you love, you grieve. It's as simple and natural as that. It's better to let those feelings come out in healthy ways now than to have them surface in unhealthy ways later on. You cannot not grieve."

~ Kenneth Haugk

Kenneth Haugk explains our natural tendency to want to avoid the pain of grief. "There are many reasons why people have difficulty grieving. Attempting to resist" [19] or bury the pain can only delay grief for so long.

Denial affects most people at some point after losing a loved one, although it may present itself differently, given the person's individual makeup. In my mind, the word "denial" indicates the idea of disbelief. While some people actually experience some form of disbelief for a period of time, denial is better described as a lack of acceptance or willingness to face one's loss.

Shock and Denial

In my research I discovered that most people who write on the subject of grief lump denial and shock together. In the early days following a death—especially sudden death—we naturally experience an inability to believe someone died. In that instance, shock hits, and it takes a while for reality to sink in. I assume experts put shock and denial together for that reason.

People in shock often appear to function rather normally. Their friends and family often assume such people live in denial. Some get stuck there, though, which leads to an unhealthy existence. A person who gets trapped in denial rarely remains in shock. That's why I prefer to separate shock and denial.

Early Denial

Immediately after the death of a loved one, we feel some form of disbelief. When Brian died, I understood in my head that he died, but I couldn't comprehend what that meant for me long term. I couldn't believe my life suddenly existed without him. We could call that denial, but I really consider it more a form of shock.

If Brian wasn't in bed, he almost always lounged in his chair in our bedroom during the last months of his life. The kids and I habitually ran down the hall to share with him news of our day. After his death we caught ourselves halfway down the hall before remembering the bedroom sat empty. Even years later, I find myself wanting to pick up the phone to tell him things—about the kids who are now mostly grown, or even about Howard and me.

Rather than denial, I would consider these experiences more a reaction to habits or routine. We just don't easily walk away from the routines that naturally occurred because of their presence in our daily lives.

Denial Type

Many live in some form of denial because they need to fit in with others. Teenagers especially typify this scenario. Awkwardness accompanies the subject of death.

My children's friends pitied them and acted strangely when the subject of their dad's death came up. Others simply ignored them and literally walked away. Dealing with other people's reactions, rudeness, and lack of compassion made it too painful for them to talk, even to their friends, about their dad's death. To this day, they find it difficult to share with new friends. They catch themselves avoiding the subject until someone asks why they refer to their dad in the past tense.

Those who find it difficult to share their feelings stay in denial for longer periods than others. These people "put on a happy face" no matter what rages within. They do their best to hide their feelings completely. For these people, the thought of experiencing the pain seems unbearable, so they literally pretend to be just fine. Some prefer to lie to themselves because they cannot bear to fall apart.

After Jordyn lost her son to cancer, she found it difficult to face the pain of her loss. She regularly says, "I feel Billy's presence around me. I talk to him all the time." Man, I wish I could say that! I constantly felt Brian's *absence* in *my* life, and if I ever spoke to him, he never responded. What a lonely existence—experiencing a one-way relationship. This poor lady's assertion that she feels her son's presence represents denial. I also believe her perception misrepresents biblical theology.

God's presence exists all around us, but not the presence of the dead. After all, if we could call on the dead, why would we need God in the midst of our pain?

Danger of Denial

Sadly, brilliant performances of pretense suffocate the grief process, often creating more problems, including health issues, PTSD, a hot temper, impatience, and other debilitating consequences.

Grief naturally follows the death of a loved one. Grief requires expression of emotion, but if a person can't allow himself to cry or talk about his pain, the healing process cannot take place. The longer we put off allowing ourselves to grieve, the more we risk getting stuck in denial.

Everything I read says that denying our feelings of grief will come back and bite us, and usually not at a convenient time.

Only fourteen months after Brian died, well-meaning friends regularly put pressure on me to date. The truth is, as I entered the worst point in my grief, others thought it time for me to "move on." Highly offended by this lack of compassion, I wanted to scream. Believe me, your grief will not end with the first anniversary of your loved one's death. Take my advice and allow yourself to openly grieve—at least during the socially acceptable period of time.

Please understand. It "is actually a sign of strength [rather than weakness] to express your emotions."[20]

Help to Others

When we pretend we carry no pain, we do our friends, and even the dead, a disservice. Why not show your friends your bleeding wound and teach them how to treat people who carry the burden of loss? When it's their turn to grieve, they will appreciate your candor. Make it your responsibility to graciously prepare your friends and family members by honestly sharing your anguish.

I found myself surprised and angry that so few people ever really talked to me about the pain of loss or even the process of death before Brian died. If people in my life had talked more about the challenges and pain of their losses, maybe I would have been better equipped.

Small Quantities and Safe People

Now, that said, life happens. We can't put everything aside and shout to the world that we walk around with a gaping wound. Sometimes we must hold it together for a job, for school, or for those who can't handle it.

Think *time* and *place*. In certain situations we must express our grief in spurts and, obviously, in the right place. Yet still, as the years go by, splashes of grief will continue to pour down upon us. The danger comes when we stuff our grief and don't allow ourselves to express it, even in small quantities, to safe people.

THE FOG

"At other times [grief] feels like being mildly drunk, or concussed. There is a sort of invisible blanket between the world and me. I find it hard to take in what anyone says. Or perhaps, hard to want to take it in. It is so uninteresting."

~C. S. Lewis, *A Grief Observed*

Referred to by many as numbness, I prefer to call this feeling a fog. Personally, I resented the word "numb." Although some people do say they feel numb, I did not feel numb. I felt enormous pain—physical pain, as well as emotional pain. Webster defines "numb" as "void of emotion; indifferent." But "fog" Webster defines as "a state of confusion or bewilderment."

Protection

The fog-like state of grief usually follows shock and hangs around much longer. Like shock, this fog also exists for our protection, although it feels like a nuisance. It shields us from experiencing the full force of the pain, though likely we experience more pain than we did in shock. Going-through-the-motions may be a better description of this state.

Some days I struggled to just lift one leg after the other to make the motions of walking. I remember walking someone to the door at my house and thinking what an exhausting effort it took to simply form steps. Concentration seemed impossible at times.

I couldn't focus to read scripture. I settled with one verse. I turned on the TV but couldn't follow the story line. I did somehow write feelings and frustrations in my journal, though they were certainly not eloquent. I also found I could sometimes read books about grief, probably out of desperation for answers to my misery. And I played Solitaire. Lots of Solitaire.

To this day, my children will tell you I formed an addiction to Solitaire. What a time waster! The truth? I couldn't concentrate, so I filled the blankness with Solitaire. It helped the hours pass. One can play Solitaire mindlessly, after all.

Life Goes On

In the midst of the fog, life must go on, even though we can't seem to function normally, and we wish the world would stop. In one sense my life came to a screeching halt, and yet I kept going, even if I hung on by only a thread.

Still blanketed in a fog, I had to address the business of closing out Brian's life while I dealt with the inability to think straight, difficulty sleeping, feelings of nausea and exhaustion. When my body wanted to collapse, I dragged myself to activities and sporting events for the kids' sakes. Everywhere I went, I wanted to hide, but I couldn't. Life—for others—continued marching on all around me.

A ringing phone presented the "threat" of a caller to whom I had to respond. But I didn't trust my emotions. I felt stuck in a crazy nightmarish dream, while the rest of the world scurried about me living life to the fullest.

Grace

Friends and loved ones tend to offer grace freely while we stumble about in a fog-like state. When we mess up at work, they excuse it and let it go because they understand that loss derails even the best of us. Unfortunately, the average person willingly extends this grace for only about a year.

When the Fog Lifts

I counted down the months to the end of the first year, thinking, "If I can just get through the first year, I might make it." I experienced moments when it felt like I could function almost normally, but this heavy weight of dense fog constantly loomed over, threatening to engulf me at any moment.

I didn't anticipate the vulture that swooped in as year two began. The fog lifted, and reality slapped me in the face. I managed to survive a year without Brian—an entire year without my best friend and companion. But suddenly, I was tasked with facing the *rest of my life* without him. At this same time, it became apparent that others expected me to "move on." I could barely move at all, though, for the reality of death sucked the life completely out of me.

> Because of the Lord's great love we are not consumed, for his compassions never fail.
>
> *Lamentations 3:22*

THE BIG "W"

"The self I once was cannot find its old place to land. It is homeless now."

~Jerry Sittser

I n one traumatic moment I moved from married status to widowed. No one earns this status willingly, nor do we wear it proudly. The title "widow" imposes itself upon us when our love is forcefully snatched from us by death. It throws us into a pit of darkness, sadness, loneliness, and confusion. And, just like that, stripped of our privacy, we lay bare for the world to watch.

Poster Child

Everyone I knew, as well as everyone *they* knew, it seemed, was aware of my new widowed status. When the kids and I walked into church, the elementary school, even the pharmacy, everyone watched. I felt like I walked around with a big "W" emblazoned across my chest.

Other people tend to watch the newly widowed to see how we manage. They watch to see how we behave, whether or not we fall apart in public, or if we can hold our heads high. They cannot comprehend our pain, so they watch, wondering what we feel, how they would react, and what happens now. Like it or not, we become the "poster child" for widowhood.

Compassion

Most people feel sorry for us and don't intend to stare or place pressure on us. Curiosity and compassion usually drive their behavior. Most people actually marvel that we show up because they can't imagine the pain we live with. They hurt deeply for us and cannot comprehend our life.

Forced to live the "poster child" life, I withdrew from public as much as possible. I also needed lots of alone time to cry. I attended church regularly for the sake of my children, and though I enjoyed relationships at church, I found it difficult to constantly "perform." I decided to use the platform as an opportunity to teach others how to minister to those who suffer. I honestly shared my pain.

Understanding

The first time I saw Susanna at church after her husband's death I made my way over to give her a big hug. She framed my face with her hands like a picture and pronounced, "I see you clearly. I understand you now!" This friend had watched from the sidelines with compassion, but now she could fully relate.

Loss of Privacy

I felt watched in public and also felt as if I'd lost my privacy at home. Out of kindness and compassion people wanted to help. I imagine if no one offered to help, my feelings might've been hurt. As it was, though, I couldn't deal with all the well-wishers who offered assistance.

All I wanted was privacy. I didn't want people in my home cleaning or bringing meals. I didn't want people in my yard mowing or on my rooftop fixing the gutters. More than any other time in my life, I needed space.

I wanted to grieve in private at home. It wasn't pretty, and I didn't want people showing up unannounced to witness my messy grief. I also needed to figure out how to cope with my new roles of single parent and head of household.

Honesty

Although I wanted privacy, I believed in honesty. Be honest when others ask how you are doing, even if you cry. Find a way to answer in short form. For example, "I'm doing well, considering." Sadly, most really don't want the details of your pain. If they want to know and understand more, they will ask questions.

Tell your closest friends how they can pray for you. If they say something hurtful, gently explain how their insensitivity hurts.

Openly share your grief for two reasons: People need to know how to understand and encourage those who hurt; and they need to prepare should they one day walk your path.

Some people feel we shouldn't share our pain with anyone. I disagree. We do no favors to others who hurt if we pretend we don't hurt. My Sunday school teacher's wife thanked me for my honesty. She said it helped her understand and gave her an example to follow should she find herself in the same situation.

God has given strength, and he will continue to give you strength if you trust in him. What a blessing to share with others how God meets us even in our despair.

> But we have this treasure in jars of clay to show that this all-surpassing power is from God and not from us. We are hard pressed on every side, but not crushed; perplexed, but not in despair; persecuted, but not abandoned; struck down, but not destroyed.
>
> *2 Corinthians 4:7–9*

VISITING THE GRAVE

"I felt as if a bait-and-switch had been pulled on me; I'd gone there longing to feel close to Hope, but it rarely worked out that way. Instead of relieving my pain, these visits merely punctuated it."

~Nancy Guthrie

Some people never visit the grave of their loved one, while others practically live there. My friend, Hazel, admits to visiting her son's grave every day for five years. In retrospect, she acknowledges her habit as unhealthy. But at the time she couldn't help herself.

Healing or Not

Everyone's needs are different. Some people can process their grief at home or with friends, while others find it cathartic to process their grief at the cemetery. I talked to a widower recently who said he'd visited the cemetery only once since the day he buried his wife. His point: "She's not there." According to the survey I conducted, this viewpoint is more common than I realized. Many spouses don't visit the cemetery for the very same reason. Others live in a different town or state, making it impossible to visit often.

I visited Brian's grave regularly the first few years. We buried Brian close to my kids' schools. I often stopped by after dropping them off at school in the morning. Home offered too many distractions, and I found it hard to focus on prayer. At the cemetery, I could stop for a while. I just sat there, read the scripture on the marker, and prayed through tears. Usually the only one there, I could "bleed out," as my friend says. It's also socially acceptable to cry at the cemetery.

The fact that Brian couldn't respond to me when I sat on his grave actually aided my healing process. The emptiness drew me to the Lord and acted as a reality check, declaring my relationship with Brian to be over this side of heaven. While sitting on his grave one day, I recognized the fact that if I wanted to experience a love like the one I shared with him, it had to include someone else.

Healthy or Not

I encourage you to think about your reasons for going or not going to the cemetery. If you try to avoid the pain by not visiting, then you may need to force yourself to go and face it. Purposely avoiding the pain proves unwise.

If you go to the cemetery because you feel obligated to your spouse, or because you feel guilty, then maybe you should allow yourself to stay home.

Flowers or Not

Of course there's nothing wrong with taking flowers every time you go to the cemetery, especially if you can afford it. I often felt sad that certain graves were never adorned with flowers. On the other hand, we must realize that the idea of taking flowers comes from our culture and makes the living feel better. The deceased don't care.

When I take flowers, I try not to spend much money on them. Brian would've told me to buy myself something instead. Certainly, if you struggle financially, don't spend much money on flowers. You can pick wild flowers, buy one single flower, or if the cemetery allows, put some fake flowers there that will last longer.

Mine or Not

If you live too far from your loved one's grave but feel the need to visit, "borrow" someone else's grave. It feels a little different, but it can give you some sense of peace. My dad is buried in West Virginia, and I live in Texas. One day before Brian died, I felt the need to visit my dad's grave, but doing so proved impossible. I chose instead to visit the grave of my friend's son. I took some flowers to place on her son's grave and cried over her loss as well as my own.

Beyond the Grave

"Our greatest comfort at the grave is the truth that for those who know and love Christ, our final destiny is not the grave—it is glory. As you stand by the grave, grab hold by faith to the promise of resurrection."[21]

As author David Guthrie points out, the scripture says "If all we get out of Christ is a little inspiration for a few short years, we're a pretty sorry lot. But the truth is that Christ has been raised up, the first in a long legacy of those who are going to [be raised]. . . . It's resurrection, resurrection, always resurrection, that undergirds what I do and say, the way I live" (1 Cor.15: 19–20, 32, MSG).[22]

For those who believe in Christ we have the hope of the resurrection—that one day we will see our loved ones again. We will know them and enjoy life with them on the New Earth where God the Father will wipe away every tear from our eyes.

He will wipe every tear from their eyes. There will be no more death or mourning or crying or pain, for the old order of things has passed away.

Revelation 21:4

GRIEF DIFFERENCES

"Grief can't be shared. Everyone carries it alone. His own burden in his own way."

~Anne Morrow Lindbergh

People grieve differently. While it may seem a simple statement, one which makes perfect sense, actually maneuvering the maze of needs and emotions proves a difficult challenge. After all, we've lost our spouse, our love. The way we grieve, how much we grieve, and how long we grieve depends on many things: the relationship we shared with our love, our individual personality, the circumstances of his/her death, and so much more. Others who grieve for the same person will likely express their pain in completely different ways.

A young child will grieve differently than a teen or an adult child because of the age difference, as well as their relationship to the deceased. We all express grief in our own individual way.

Normal?

All grief is normal. One person may cry incessantly while another won't cry at all. One may express anger, and another withdraws completely. Some sleep too much. Others can't sleep at all. Many widows need to talk. They need to talk about their spouse, how he or she died, and what their days are like all alone. But some don't want to broach the subject at all. They cope by pretending everything remains the same. Teenagers, in particular, tend to act like nothing happened. They can't bear to stick out in a crowd, so they act just fine on the outside while screaming on the inside.

Overwhelming

Wow! As I write, I become more and more aware of the enormity of the grief we face in the midst of the worst nightmare of our lives. No wonder we feel completely crazy, overwhelmed, frustrated, and angry.

What to do

My mom used to say that when we were little and she felt completely overwhelmed, she would tell herself she could make it ten minutes. At the end of those ten minutes, she told herself she could make it another ten minutes. Sometimes that's the best we can do.

At times I longed for bedtime when I could just crash and, although I had trouble sleeping, no pressing matters required my attention. The silence of the night offered not only a reprieve from daily responsibilities, but also the reality of complete and utter loneliness. During these moments I cried out to the Almighty God for strength to make it just one more day.

> "One day at a time, sweet Jesus, is all I'm asking from you. Lord, give me the strength to do every day what I have to do. Yesterday's gone, sweet Jesus, and tomorrow may never be mine. Lord, help me today, show me the way, one day at a time."[23]
>
> ~Marijohn Wilkin and Kris Kristofferson

> "Day by day and with each passing moment, strength I find to meet my trials here. Trusting in my Father's wise bestowment, I've no cause for worry or for fear."[24]
>
> ~Lina Sandell

CLOSING OUT A LIFE

"The last straw was the statement that I needed to send in an original death certificate with this set of papers."

~H. Norman Wright

The paperwork, the phone calls, sending out death certificates . . . Will it ever end?

When new life begins and a baby enters the world, we sign a few papers. The hospital staff files the paperwork, and we take our baby home. The birth certificate and social security number arrive in the mail.

When someone dies, however, we not only grieve, but it seems we must notify a million different people and businesses. This requires organization, time, presence of mind, and energy—none of which we naturally possess after the death of a loved one.

The amount of work it takes to close out a life, especially the main bread-winner's, overwhelms us. During emotionally stable times, this kind of business invokes stress and requires great effort. But under the duress of grief, dealing with the business aspects of death can suck the life out of us.

You've likely already made some of the most difficult decisions, including which funeral home to use, whether to cremate or bury your spouse, picking out an urn or a casket, and making funeral arrangements. You made it this far.

Now, you can—and you must—address the business of closing out your love's life. Frustration explodes everywhere during this process. Allow yourself break-downs. Allow yourself to put things off for a day or so if necessary. But force yourself to take care of the business that requires your attention.

Immediate Advice

Thankfully, a close family friend walked me through the first details of finding a financial advisor and going to the Social Security office after Brian died. I didn't know where to begin on my own. If you don't know anyone experienced in these things, try to find a friend willing to go to some of these places with you to help think things through and gather information.

The most important items to address:

1. Death Certificates:

You will need lots of death certificates, likely more than the regularly provided ones. The funeral home should provide these. Ask the funeral director for extras and just pay for them up front. This saves the hassle of going back for more if you need them later.

Scan one into the computer, as some companies will accept an e-mailed or faxed version. This saves you having to put so many in the mail. Do what makes your life as simple as possible. When a death certificate is required, ask if you can send a copy via e-mail or if they will accept a photocopy. E-mailing requires a simple click of the button and you're done. Mailing a photocopy allows you to save your certified copies in case they become necessary.

2. Financial:

The two biggest questions:

- What to do with the life insurance money?
- What to do regarding finances if no life insurance money exists?

If your spouse provided for you and your family financially, you are very blessed. Do not waste the gift.

Before making any investment decisions, I highly recommend Dana Barfield's book, *My Friend Just Lost Her Husband*. A financial advisor himself, he found most of his widowed clients lost in a maze of confusion. Because he discovered most widows lean heavily on close friends, he wrote a book to teach friends how to help their widowed friend find a good financial advisor. At the back, he includes a helpful section on investments.

Before investing money with a friend, consider the following:

- Do you want that person to know your personal financial business? Awkwardness can ensue when friends know your private financial information. Be extremely careful whom you choose.
- Would it ruin the friendship if it came time to switch advisors? In other words, if you had to fire your friend, would you be sorry?

- Do you feel comfortable dealing regularly with his/her gender? I didn't want to talk to someone else's husband about my finances. I felt more comfortable dealing with a woman.

- Can your friendship handle conflict if disagreements arise?

How to choose a financial adviser:

- Prepare a list of questions to ask during your initial meeting.

- Interview people from different companies.

- Ask widowed friends and those who manage their finances well who they would recommend.

- Take as much time as you need to determine what to do with your money (if you haven't already invested).

- Become informed, even if you feel good about your current situation. Circumstances may eventually necessitate changes to your plan.

If you must quickly get a job in order to make ends meet, I am very sorry. Being forced into such a situation may cause you to experience anger toward your spouse for not providing adequately for you. This is normal, expected, and very difficult. Enlist friends to help you in this circumstance, as well, and ask the Lord to provide. Most churches have benevolence funds and may willingly help until you can support yourself.

3. Social Security

No matter what your age or sex, as long as your spouse worked at all, you likely qualify for Social Security death benefits. Go to www.socialsecurity.gov; click on Survivors; click on Apply for Survivors Benefits. Funeral homes typically report deaths to the social security office, which makes this process easier for you.

4. Health Insurance

If your health insurance comes through your employer, no problem. You must simply report the death to your Human Resources department if your spouse was covered under your policy.

If your spouse's employer covered your health insurance, you must deal with this issue immediately. Hopefully, if you contact your spouse's Human Resources department, they will handle the transition for you. Usually COBRA takes over automatically, at least for the rest of the calendar year. In October, find someone to help you make the decision regarding your health insurance for the following year.

I suffered a nightmare trying to get the proper information transferred over to COBRA. I continually received medical bills that should have been paid one hundred percent. Hopefully, you will have a smoother transition. The only way to handle problems? Hound the customer service employees until they get it right. Problems completely drain our emotional energy, but we must persevere.

Breaking down on the phone, sobbing, I finally dumped my entire story on one quite unfortunate customer service representative. I wailed about the pain of loss, and the fact that these kinds of problems only make matters worse. Amazingly, I received no more bills after that. I imagine she didn't want to hear from me again.

5. Changing Names

When we make large purchases with our spouse, most of us assume listing the property in both names solves all problems if something happens to one of us. While it may keep the property out of probate, we must still legally remove the name of the deceased from certain documents and accounts.

The home mortgage, car titles, bank accounts, investment accounts, and the like require more work than utility companies and credit cards. List all accounts and inquire as to each one's requirements with regard to changing the owner from both names to just yours. Friends can make the initial calls for you. I did this for a friend who lost her husband before Brian's death. Sometimes they wanted to speak to her, but she found it much easier if I made the call first. Usually a death certificate along with a letter suffices.

6. Notification of Death

Yet another emotionally draining experience is notifying businesses of the fact that your love died. Similar to changing names on documents and loans, you must also notify accounts on which your spouse was identified as the primary owner that you will now take responsibility for them (utility bills, credit cards, bank accounts, and so forth).

Some utility companies don't really care who owns the account, as long as they get paid. In that case, there's no rush to deal with those accounts. Credit card companies, however, will likely ask you to close out the account and open your own. Address this carefully, especially if you can't qualify on your own for a credit card.

My recommendation:

- Make a list of companies that need notification.
- Determine which ones are a priority.
- Compose a basic letter.
- Save the letter on your computer so you only need to change the business name, address, and the account number.
- Attack the list little by little—or all at once if your emotional capacity allows.
- Keep a copy of every letter.

7. Credit Cards

Toward the end of his life, it angered me that credit card companies happily accepted my payments, but representatives wouldn't speak to me without Brian's approval even when he was barely coherent. Sadly, greedy people in sick marriages caused this problem for those of us dealing with death and dying.

As mentioned above, credit card companies often require a cancellation instead of name change if you aren't the primary cardholder. If you need to keep a credit card, make sure you can qualify on your own before informing the bank of your spouse's death. Do not go on a spending spree with it, though. If you choose to hang on to a credit card for which you can't personally qualify, keep in mind that when the need arises to call the credit card company, they will likely cancel your account at that point.

If, by some chance, you insured your credit cards, check the details to see when to make a claim. Don't take my word for it, but likely the fine print indicates you must make the claim within the first year. Many people forget they own the insurance and never file—or possibly your spouse purchased it without your knowledge. If your card carries a balance the insurance policy pays off the debt. Check all cards to see if insurance exists. Do *not* forget to file the claim!

8. Probate

If your spouse's estate requires probate, you will likely need a lawyer. In some instances, the bank will freeze your assets and not allow access to your own bank account. Find a trusted lawyer and rally your friends and family to help.

9. Bank

Apparently Social Security notifies your bank when a person dies. I didn't know this. It did not come up until I tried to sell my house almost a year after Brian's death. My lawyer changed the title into my name the night before we removed Brian from life support. Because of this, I naturally assumed all was well. But my bank wouldn't accept the wire from the title company when the transaction completed. It took days, numerous trips to the bank, lots of tears, and one compassionate bank manager to fix the problem.

10. Legal Matters

- Update your **will** now if your number one beneficiary died.

- Name a **Power of Attorney** in case you become incapacitated.

- Obtain a **Living Will**, which states your desires with regard to your health.

- Consider adding at least one adult child, parent, or someone trustworthy to your **bank account** in case you become incapacitated.

Accomplishments

So many frustrations come with the business of closing out your spouse's life. Hang in there. Take breaks. Throw your fits of frustration in private. Cry out to the Lord. Then try tackling it again. You will find great relief and satisfaction each time you mark one of these details off your list.

God shows his faithfulness by giving us the ability to muster enough strength for the tough tasks. By accomplishing them, we gain the confidence that we *can* do even the hard things with God's help.

> But he said to me, "My grace is sufficient for you, for my power is made perfect in weakness. Therefore I will boast all the more gladly about my weaknesses, so that Christ's power may rest on me. That is why, for Christ's sake, I delight in weaknesses, in insults, in hardships, in persecutions, in difficulties. For when I am weak, then I am strong."
>
> *2 Corinthians 12:9–10*

THE FIRST YEAR

"Of the widow's countless death-duties there is really just one that matters: on the first anniversary of her husband's death the widow should think 'I kept myself alive.'"

~Joyce Carol Oates

The first year tends to be a blur. Emotions fly all over the place. Some days we feel perfectly normal, and other days we can hardly get out of bed. Initially, it can feel like your spouse has gone on an extended vacation. We miss them, but it takes a while for reality to sink in.

Ups and Downs

Two months after his wife died, Juan told me he doesn't cry at all some days, which leaves him feeling guilty. Other days, he can hardly stop crying, and he feels guilty about that. He can go visit his great-granddaughter and enjoy himself without feeling his enormous loss. Yet, other days he can barely function. In one conversation with him, I heard just about every emotion possible.

Confusion

Juan rambled on about his loss and tried to explain his condition. His emotions were all over the place. He described one scenario and contradicted himself in the next sentence. He said he had not experienced any anger, and yet in a previous conversation, he confessed anger that made him feel ashamed. His thoughts and feelings collided with one another, and he couldn't sort them out.

Knowing his cancer would take his life, Ray prayed that his wife Candice would remarry after his death. Six months after he died, Candice felt confused. She wept while reminiscing about her husband. She missed him terribly. In the same conversation, she gushed over another man she'd met who impressed her. Although her grief was still too raw to consider remarriage, she longed for the answer to her husband's prayer, and her emotions betrayed her.

For this very reason, most counselors don't recommend remarriage within the first two years after a death or divorce. Emotions volley back and forth constantly, causing much confusion. In this state of mind, a person could easily make an unwise choice. See the section "Don't Be Stupid" for more on this subject.

Business

In the midst of all of the confusion and emotional roller coasters we ride, we find ourselves stuck with mountains of paperwork and business we must attend to. On the one hand, this gives us something to do. On the other hand, we find ourselves unable to think straight. This makes the business of closing out our spouse's life a heavy burden. Find a friend who can help with this if possible. See also the chapter, "Closing out a Life."

Survival Mode

We find ourselves in the midst of survival mode after the death of our spouse. Every moment we hang on, feverishly trying to survive the pain, the work, or the monotony. In the middle of the emotional ups and downs, we still must cook, manage single parenting, deal with a leaky roof, or survive the silence of the house, an empty chair, and an empty bed. It all feels very overwhelming.

As I mentioned earlier, I counted down the months to the end of the first year, mistakenly believing if I could just survive the first year, I'd make it. Reality hit in the second year, and I crashed into depression.

Part Two

WHEN DEATH SUCKS THE LIFE OUT OF YOU

Section One

REALITIES

FAMILIAR BECOMES UNFAMILIAR

"Nothing is as it was. Even the familiar becomes unfamiliar."

~H. Norman Wright

O
h, my goodness! All of a sudden nothing seems normal. Literally everything changes. What a relief to see that Norman Wright used the same words I used to describe his grief.

About six weeks after Brian's death, my friend Josh asked me how I was doing. When the tears welled up and he could clearly see my emotion, he asked what made my life hard. I wanted to shout, "Duh!" Instead, I paused to think, but no words came that could adequately express the pain I felt. I summed it up in one huge understatement, "*Everything!*"

Family Gatherings

My in-laws hosted a typical family dinner, but it didn't play out as typical. I walked into the dining room to sit in my normal spot by Brian, but of course he wouldn't attend this dinner. Where should I sit? A moment of inexpressible grief crushed me over the "simple" matter of where to sit. Sitting in the familiar spot seemed un-bearably lonely. I chose, instead, to sit across the table in what now felt completely unfamiliar.

What typically qualified as usual conversation suddenly didn't feel familiar either. It suddenly dawned on me that I was no longer part of a two-person team; I now existed as a fractured one.

Entertainment

Brian and I always held hands (yes, even after nineteen years of marriage). Friends who participated in a local community theatre invited the kids and me to their play one night. I managed well during the first half, but when I sat down for the second half of the play, I reached over to take Brian's hand. Tears overflowed as I realized once again that even the "simple" experience of attending a play had become foreign and so terribly painful.

Shopping

Overnight, the grocery store converts to a stranger. More than once I reached to grab the box of cereal Brian liked, but he no longer needed it. I glanced around the store. Everyone else appeared to go about their business pushing carts, some talking away on their phones, while I stared into space, practically paralyzed—yet attempting to remain composed. Every item I once bought for Brian now turned on me as if an enemy, harshly sneering reminders of my loss.

Men whose wives did all of the shopping find themselves lost in a jungle of boxes, bags, bottles, and baskets. The temptation to bolt grows while the thought of making meals just doesn't seem important anymore. Eating out quickly becomes the easy choice.

New Roles

Tasks your spouse managed without much thought now sit incomplete or you must figure out how to accomplish them. After Ann died, Howard tried to follow a recipe for potato soup. The recipe called for six cups of cooked potatoes. Okay. Baking potatoes, new potatoes, sweet potatoes, or Idaho potatoes? Secondly, do you skin them, chop them, or mash them? Boil, bake, or microwave?

Just following a recipe conquered him. If the recipe called for half an onion, what was he supposed to do with the rest of the onion? He eventually created his own recipes using amounts that made sense to him.

Opposite-Sex Relationships

Women and men alike share the question: How much do I lean on friends of the opposite sex? It is uncomfortable—and unwise—to open up to someone else's spouse about your needs. Unexpectedly, we suddenly need the help of someone else's spouse to either give kitchen advice or fix a leaky faucet.

Exercising caution in this area is vital. You are vulnerable. At the very least, make sure your friend knows her spouse plans to help you. Consider asking that friend to accompany her husband to your home. Make sure at least one of your children stays home, or invite another friend or neighbor to come over while he's there.

Cora hired a family friend to do lots of handyman chores for her after her husband died. He often encouraged her by talking about her husband, but she felt his behavior teetered on the verge of inappropriate. He engaged her children in conversation and treated them with kindness. She appreciated that. They needed godly men to speak into their lives.

The problem? He felt too comfortable hugging her. A few times he even hugged her in her bedroom. A married man should never hug another woman in her home with neither spouse present. She ended up hiring someone else for other jobs, not because she found herself attracted to him, but because she no longer felt safe.

I found myself completely vulnerable outside of my husband's umbrella. Men often hugged me at church without their wives present. I cannot express how awkward that feels to a newly single woman. I'm sure they had pure intentions; they merely wanted to encourage a poor widow who couldn't receive hugs from her husband. These men didn't understand that their kind gestures put a "poor widow" on guard, feeling exposed and unsafe.

Sam told me he couldn't stand all of the widows flirting with him. As a widower, he was now an eligible bachelor, and the women practically fought for his attention. They manipulated his time, brought him meals, batted their eyes, and maneuvered to get close to him. Disgusted, he wanted to hide.

We widows need kind helpers who behave appropriately. Plenty of vulnerable widows will respond to a kind person of the opposite sex, and then both end up in a huge dilemma. Do not allow any behavior that feels inappropriate, even if only intended as kindness.

Help

Accept help from others for a while, if you can handle it. If it works for you, let people bring meals or clean for you, but manage the assistance on your terms. Feel free to accept or reject any offer of help based on your needs. A new widow named Grace comfortably left her door unlocked while her friends came and went in order to help. It didn't bother her at all. Me? I needed privacy.

My kids tired of our tumultuous and chaotic life. They grew weary of eating other people's food. Well-wishers begged us to let them help. But after a time, we simply wanted solitude. I finally relented and began accepting restaurant gift cards, as I could not bear to greet people at the door. By sending gift cards, others could feel they eased our burden, while we could choose to go out, pick up food, cook, or just stay at home and eat cereal.

Withdrawal

I couldn't meet people at the door to receive meals or help of any sort. I didn't want to make conversation or answer questions. I needed to gather my little chickens under my wings and hide out in my safe haven. I couldn't handle people showing up at my house to help, especially unannounced. Normally a social person, I needed to withdraw.

Solution

No answers or solutions exist for the dilemma of the unfamiliar other than to just hang in there. We must simply hang on, keep trudging, and figure it out over time. Eventually, the unfamiliar becomes a new familiar.

Although everything in life turns completely upside down, Jesus remains the same. We can, in the very least, hold on to that promise.

Jesus Christ is the same yesterday, today, and forever.

Hebrews 13:8

NO CELL PHONES IN HEAVEN

"Grief is love turned into an eternal missing."

~Rosamund Lupton, Sister

"Oh, Brian, I just want to talk to you!" I yelled out loud in the car one day. Though eight full months had gone by, I still needed his listening ear, his encouraging words, and his input. I had survived eight months without him, and I could stand it no longer.

Habits

Since Brian was sick for so long, my kids and I habitually came in the door and went straight to the bedroom to tell him about our day. After his death we caught ourselves heading down the hall before remembering he no longer occupied the bedroom. I noticed myself making sure I carried my cell phone with me when I left the house in case he needed me.

I reached for the phone to call him so many times! I talked to him about everything. I told him once during our marriage that I could never have an affair because I'd end up telling him about it. Now, suddenly, I couldn't communicate with him at all. I just wanted to tell him about the kids. I needed his input. I wanted to share my pain. Or tell him who recently got married, pregnant, or died. It took a long time for my brain to register that Brian no longer existed anywhere in my world.

When Howard and I started dating, I caught myself wanting to dial Brian's cell phone to tell him what God provided for me in his absence. I wanted Brian at my wedding, as strange as that sounds.

Enormous Loss

Soon after Brian received his terminal diagnosis, I began to cry one night after we went to bed. He held me in his arms. The tears turned to sobs as it dawned on me that he could not comfort me after his death when I would need him most.

The one person from whom I received the most comfort in this life could no longer comfort me in my time of greatest need. I realized how often I went to him, how often we shared things, how much I relied on him emotionally, how often he made me laugh. I longed to hear his voice and constantly yearned for a conversation with him. No communication device reaches into heaven, however, except that which goes through the Father.

I shared with a friend once how I longed for just one more conversation with Brian. I needed to know he approved of my parenting. Amazingly, the Lord graciously gave me a dream in which Brian got into my car and told me how well he thought I handled the children. What a wonderful gift!

Where to Turn

The most important thing I learned in my lonely moments: I must turn to the Lord. Friends and family may be wonderfully helpful, but no single person can meet my every need. Brian couldn't even do that.

A friend asked me once if I talk to Brian. Yes, every now and then I blurt something out to him, but he can no longer respond to me.

I needed to find my comfort, grace, wisdom, and direction from the Lord. He alone can meet my every need.

> O Lord my God, I called to you for *help* and
> > you *healed* me....
> Sing to the Lord, you saints of his;
> Praise his Holy name
> For his anger lasts only a moment
> But his favor lasts a lifetime;
> *Weeping* may remain for a night
> But *rejoicing* comes in the morning....
> *You* turned my *wailing* into *dancing*!
> *You* removed my sackcloth and
> Clothed me with *joy*,
> *that* my *heart* may *sing* to *you* and not be silent.
> O *Lord* my God, I will give you thanks forever.

Psalm 30:2, 4–5, 11–12

(*emphasis mine*)

In You, Lord, I take *refuge.*

Let me never be put to *shame.*

...be my rock of *refuge.*

Psalm 31:1, 2
(emphasis mine)

LOSSES

"Each substance of grief hath twenty shadows."

~ William Shakespeare, Richard II

The death of a spouse, or any loved one for that matter, encompasses numerous losses. The word "loss" means "deprivation."[1] We have been deprived, not only of the person whom we love, but all that he or she represented to us. For many married couples, all of our hopes and dreams tend to be wrapped up in our spouse—as well as all of the joys and sorrows that came with being married to him.

Death severs our relationship, which means everything involved in the relationship cuts off as well. This amputation leaves us alone to complete the rest of our lives without this person's love, encouragement, help, support, criticism (whether helpful or not), and on it goes.

Best Friend

Brian was my very best friend. I love and appreciate many close friends, but suddenly the one person to whom I always made the first call could not answer the phone, and I felt completely alone.

Brian warred with cancer for almost nine years. Although he lived with limitations, I couldn't comprehend how to function without him. His health rendered him incapable of helping much with tasks around the house, but he always listened to me, held me in his arms when I needed a hug, and sat ready with just the right joke to make me laugh, eager to express words of encouragement to the kids and me.

Brian rarely said anything negative. If he ever complained about his illness, he apologized for it. I used to tell him that for a man with little emotion, he carried an enormous amount of compassion for others. I lost my best friend when he died.

Dreams

With the loss of our love, we also lose all of the plans, dreams and expectations for our future together, as well as for our kids. Our lives suddenly come to a screeching halt. Instead of making that trip to Colorado together or moving to Florida for retirement, our plans require reevaluation and reconsideration. Regardless of the decisions we make—either positive or negative—our future has changed.

Brian made it his goal to walk his daughter down the aisle at her wedding. He died before her eleventh birthday. He can no longer fill the pictures in her dreams of her dad walking her down the aisle on the day she pledges herself to the love of her life. She loves her step-dad, and Howard will likely walk her down the aisle. Even so, she will feel sorrow over the absence of her dad on that day.

Whether we like it or not, grief obligates us to accept the changes our dreams must take. Jerry Sittser eloquently stated, "I remembered a past that included people I did not want to give up, and I imagined a future that excluded people I desperately wanted to keep. There is no going back to the past, which is gone forever, only going ahead to the future, which has yet to be discovered."[2]

Relationship

This side of heaven, death leaves relationships severed. This reality hit me hard one day as I sat over Brian's grave, praying and weeping. I looked up at the headstone with fresh eyes. All I have left of him are my memories, my kids, and this piece of grass that holds a stone with his name on it. What a terribly depressing revelation, and yet a necessary profundity that began the process of my healing.

As I mention under "Relationships" many, if not most, of our relationships change as a result of one death. Death changes us. We suddenly exist as one person missing a leg, yet trying to walk normally.

"You aren't the same mom you used to be!" my daughter snapped at me. How intensely insightful. I limped along, trying to keep up, striving to meet the needs of my kids, but I felt chopped in half. It affected everyone around me.

Although blessed to have friends who stuck by my side, some relationships did change. I became less social. I no longer felt as safe in certain relationships and couldn't muster the strength to pretend in others. Most people care, and they express it well, but I felt abused by many.

Too many people offered advice for my plight, about which they knew nothing. Some, completely oblivious to the emotional trauma I lived with on a daily basis, put pressure on me to date before I could see straight. I wanted friends and family to just listen, encourage, and at least try to understand. Very few people can achieve that.

Special Touch

We see couples who don't appreciate one another and our hearts ache. We see couples adoring each other and our hearts ache. We watch movies that seem to always include romance, and our hearts ache some more. How we miss being touched, but not just by anyone. We miss the touch of the one from whom we will never again be touched, and our hearts scream out in pain.

Sexual

"I thought I would never get to have sex again," Demetri admitted. With the loss of our spouse also comes the loss of our sexual relationship.

Some take sexual loss harder than others. My other friend Jake called it "just one more loss." According to my survey, it seems the elderly find this less difficult than younger widows and widowers—that is, if those who took my survey answered honestly.

The truth? Most left the sexual questions blank. This fact leads me to believe the loss of the sexual relationship hurts more than people feel comfortable admitting. See also "Don't Be Stupid" and "Sex."

Financial

Whether we profit from a great big life insurance policy, nothing at all, or somewhere in between, our financial situation typically changes as a result of our loss. Those left well-off financially often feel guilty for "benefitting" from their spouse's death. Some spend frivolously, while others hesitate to spend a dime. Shame often attacks when we catch ourselves enjoying it.

Those who don't receive benefits from a life insurance policy—and find themselves stuck in a bad financial position—can commonly feel anger. Not only did she lose her spouse, but now she must also supplement her income. Many women who spent years as homemakers suddenly must find employment, though they possess little work experience. The lack of job history on a resume makes finding a job, especially one that pays well, much more difficult. This adds stress to all other losses.

Title

To some degree, our marital status defines us. In one moment we are stripped of the title "Married." By no choice of ours, the title "Widowed" forces itself upon us. How strange it sounds to our ears, and how deeply it affects our emotional state.

Eliana announced one day on Facebook the simple words, "I am a widow." Her announcement came as a shock to most people. They felt sad and expressed compassion for her. To me, however, it represented a profound statement.

I could relate in-depth to what those words meant. I also imagine that when she typed those four words, the moment overwhelmed her and she could muster nothing more. Once again, Jerry Sittser sums it up well: "I am not a husband anymore, but neither do I perceive myself as single. . . . I am a widower, a single parent. . . . It is a confusing and peculiar identity."[3]

Normalcy

The loss of a spouse ends everything we consider normal. In one split second, our lives are forever changed and become chaotic. Every moment brings with it something new. We ache for one day of normalcy, but we don't even know how to describe such a thing anymore. And the truth is, it can take years to establish a new normal.

Parenting

If children still live at home, the widow immediately becomes a single parent. Single parenting, especially to grieving children, represents one of the most difficult tasks in the world. The responsibility of parenting rests solely on our shoulders, at a time when we just want to crawl up in a ball or hide somewhere in a hole.

The moment we become a single parent, our children become partial orphans. In essence, my children lost one parent to death and the other parent to grief. While I didn't die physically, my husband's death killed me emotionally. The death of one family member changed our entire unit. The loss of a parent robs children of their sense of safety. Their entire world turns upside down just as ours does.

The end of the losses seems to never come. At every turn, we come face-to-face with more loss, and we grieve each one. In the midst of trying to cope on a daily basis, we experience an unbearable amount of loss. No wonder grief is so terribly overwhelming!

> He will wipe every tear from their eyes. There will be no more death or mourning or crying or pain, for the old order of things has passed away.
>
> *Revelation 21:4*

HOLIDAYS/SPECIAL OCCASIONS

"The traditions and events that can add so much joy and meaning to the season are punctuated with painful, repeated reminders of our loss."

~ Nancy Guthrie

I t never ends! We manage to get through one special occasion or holiday and another one hides around the corner, waiting to ambush. And on and on it goes.

We feel like we're on the merry-go-round Patsy Cline sang about in "Oh Stop the World and Let Me Off." We grow weary of circling around the fresh grief every holiday brings. I relate well to the lyrics, *"I played the game of love and lost, so stop the world and let me off."*[4]

Birthdays, New Years, Valentine's Day, Easter, Mother's Day, Memorial Day, Graduations, Father's Day, weddings, Fourth of July, Labor Day, Halloween, Thanksgiving, Christmas, New Year's Eve, your wedding anniversary, the first and last days of school, the anniversary of our loved one's death.

We make it through one round of all of those, and the cycle starts all over again! How on earth do we manage to keep going "'round and 'round"?

Plan Ahead

First of all, begin with one holiday at a time. As each special day approaches, begin to think about how you feel and what activities or events you think you can stomach. Many of us celebrate special traditions related to these days, and the thought of carrying out those traditions without our partner may seem daunting.

Consider: Can I handle traditions this year or do I need to do something differently?

Children, whether at home or grown and out of the house, may expect things a certain way. Ask them about their needs and expectations and share your own with them.

Depending on their age, you may need to stick to some form of tradition for the sake of young children, unless they need a break as well. Small children will not understand your feelings and need everything possible to feel normal, although you can prepare them by discussing plans ahead of time. Still, sometimes we must "put on a happy face" and go through the motions for the sake of the children. Other times we can express our needs and completely alter plans.

Everyone may agree on their needs and desires, but others will express hurt and put pressure on you to do things their way. If you just cannot face it, say so.

The most difficult holidays for me were Halloween, Thanksgiving, Christmas, and the anniversary of Brian's death. I keep wanting to add to the list!

Halloween

By far, Halloween topped my list of worsts. Halloween came just three months after Brian's death, and I was intensely aware of the decay taking place in his body. Driving through the neighborhood haunted me as I saw skeletons, coffins, and grave markers. I wondered how people could take death so casually and turn it into fun. To put it lightly, I felt highly offended, to the point that I couldn't face any part of Halloween.

My daughter, on the other hand, eleven at that time, wanted to dress up as a zombie for Halloween. I owe a huge debt to my oldest son who managed to understand her needs as well as mine and took it upon himself to meet both.

My friend Carol, who lost her son five years earlier, brought dinner and hung out with me in my bedroom. Chad (17) took Nikki trick-or-treating and AJ (14) handed out candy. Carol and I laughed, cried, and hid from the outside world, while my kids joyfully participated in what nauseated me.

Holidays

Once again I will say that we all experience differences in how we handle things and in what we need. I cannot say I managed everything perfectly. Especially the first year, my children needed to do things differently, as did I. Thankfully, the four of us shared the same needs on big holidays. We just needed to band together to get through the most difficult days. We opted not to join extended family on those occasions because none of us felt up to it. The thought of joining Brian's family without him was entirely too difficult.

Brian's family doesn't easily show emotion, and I couldn't hide mine. Part of our need to separate from Brian's family on holidays came from my need to talk about Brian and feel the freedom to cry openly. I was incapable of suppressing my tears.

We must try to understand that family members often grieve in different ways than we do. Their grief also qualifies as normal and acceptable. The loving thing to do? Allow others to communicate and experience their needs while striving to manage your own. Try not to take offense if others express grief differently than you do.

You may not want to face the holidays *without* everyone around you. That is perfectly fine and normal, as well. It helps to figure out our own personal needs and then find a way to meet them without causing too much of a ruckus for others. This difficult dance takes patience and kindness. If others put pressure on you when you simply cannot find the strength, tell them kindly that you just can't do it this year. Sorry.

Thanksgiving

Our first Thanksgiving without Brian we joined friends who go to the beach every year. They graciously invited us to participate in their tradition. We flew in a small-engine plane, and the flight reminded me of my childhood days riding to boarding school in a similar airplane. En route, I reminisced with the kids about growing up as a missionary's kid. Once we arrived, my kids had a blast with their friends at the beach. I occasionally felt alone in a big crowd, but it also felt good to do something totally out of the ordinary.

I jumped into the cold water and went wakeboarding. A total change of pace infused a little joy into our sadness. It didn't take away the pain of loss, but a different atmosphere, different people, and different food and traditions helped to minimize it somewhat. In some ways it seemed more like a vacation away than like Thanksgiving, which came as a welcome relief.

Christmas

Our first Christmas after Brian's death, we stayed home and did our own thing. We all stayed in our pajamas and ate biscuits and gravy for Christmas dinner. I picked some of Brian's things I thought the kids would like and wrapped them as gifts from their dad. In the afternoon the kids decided they would feel like Brian could somehow participate in their Christmas if we went through his things.

AJ, my fourteen year old, played the clown. He put on Brian's suit, cowboy hat, and boots and performed for us. What a joy to just find the ability to laugh! Each of the kids picked out some of Brian's clothes to keep even though they would likely never fit them (they inherited their size from me). Brian towered over me at 6' 2". Our tallest son, now fully grown, stands only 5' 8" tall.

The One-Year Anniversary

What a horrific day! I wanted to skip the day altogether, but the option to skip a day doesn't exist, unfortunately. Brian's family wanted to get together, but we just couldn't do it. We were a mess—well, actually *I* was a mess. I spent the entire week before the anniversary in tears and couldn't seem to control it. The kids didn't want to dwell on the pain of the day, so I tried, for their sakes, to keep myself under some form of control. They wanted to go to the hospital where Brian died and get Frulattis, a special kind of smoothie. They wanted to relive the *good* part of the mayhem. The last month of Brian's life we daily bought Frulattis downstairs in the hospital lobby.

I made the drive with the kids to the hospital on this awful memorial day, but I could not go inside. Our compromise: the kids went in to buy the smoothies and brought them out to the car.

Special Occasions

Even though the pain slowly lessens over the years, difficult days remain. On what would've been my 24th wedding anniversary, five years after Brian's death, I wrote in my journal, "I tire of the lingering pain of loss. These days that hold meaning are so weird. On the one hand, they are simply a number, a day in time, and yet my heart breaks anew, as if the loss were fresh. I always think, 'This year I'm going to be okay,' but I have yet to experience that."

When Chad, my oldest, graduated from high school I felt immense pride in his accomplishment mixed with terrible sadness that his dad couldn't join the celebration. By the time AJ graduated, I had remarried, and this time two kids graduated the same year. Again, we were proud of both AJ and Hannah (Howard's daughter) and yet our hearts broke that her mom and his dad couldn't participate in the celebrations. Howard's oldest son, Paul, married a year after we did, and we all grieved deeply over his mother's absence.

Thankfully "special days" don't happen on a daily basis or we couldn't handle the turmoil. As time passes, we will continue to celebrate graduations, weddings, and the births of grandchildren. Although we will experience great joy, we will continue to feel lingering sadness.

Surprised by Grief

Even as I wrote the last touches of this book, grief snatched my joy. The Fourth of July. Determined to finish the book, I went to work, pouring over grief books to find just the right quotes. I wanted to make sure I didn't forget anything important.

Feelings of loss haunted me, and I couldn't figure out why the Fourth of July felt so painful. I went to bed with a heavy heart, feeling overpowered by loss. As I recounted my experience to Howard the next morning, it hit me: Brian stood on his own two feet for the last time on the Fourth of July. It was also the last day he spent at home.

I found him on the bathroom floor in the early hours of July 5. He couldn't get himself up, and between Chad and me, we couldn't budge him either. I called 911. He died three weeks later in the hospital.

Seven July Fourths have passed since then. This year, although my conscious mind hadn't made the connection, my subconscious couldn't forget. This experience is not uncommon.

> When you pass through the waters, I will be with you; And through the rivers, they will not overflow you. When you walk through the fire, you will not be scorched; nor will the flame burn you.
>
> *Isaiah 43:1–3*

Section Two

DAILY SIDE EFFECTS

FOCUS—OR LACK THEREOF

"Dear Grief: You are a rascal. You take our energy, our organizational abilities, and our brains and do strange things to them."

~ H. Norman Wright

In the months after Brian's death, I existed as a zombie cast in the starring role of my own life. I recognized the face in the mirror, but no longer knew the person staring back at me.

As mentioned before, I developed an addiction to Solitaire. Honestly, I couldn't focus on anything. I tried to read, but forgot what I just read. I tried praying but couldn't get through more than one or two sentences. When watching TV, I couldn't follow the story line. I gave up.

My solution? Solitaire. I mindlessly wasted time playing games. At least I did *something*, I thought! It also helped fill the long, monotonous hours and gave me something to do besides dwell on my sorrow.

Concentration and focus vanish in the first months after losing our spouse. Strangely, at the time we need the most focus, to handle the business of closing out a life, to function as a single parent—possibly for the first time—and to manage the household duties on our own, we find our concentration evaporates. In the midst of readjusting to so many changes, it seems nearly impossible to focus.

Friends and family may willingly help handle certain kinds of business for you. Managing tasks comes easier when someone walks us through the motions. Eventually, though, it falls on us to complete these tasks even when we find it difficult to concentrate.

No one can really tell us how to deal with this. We simply must stumble our way through while clinging to the Lord for strength. A few suggestions may help keep your sanity:

Be patient with yourself.

Acknowledge the fact that this curse lasts for a while. Embrace the idea that others will give you grace during this time, so offer yourself some grace as well.

Allow yourself bad days.

Some days are just tougher than others. Unless something really presses for completion on one of those particularly bad days, allow yourself to wallow for a while in your grief. Healthy grief cries it out. You might just feel better tomorrow because you allowed yourself some grieving time today.

Write things down.

Keep a notepad, keep notes on your phone, or whatever works for you. Writing things down takes some of the pressure off trying to remember them.

I found journaling aided in the process of completing thoughts and working through emotions. In no way do my journal entries signify well-worded prose, but in retrospect I now see the completion of things I couldn't accomplish without pen to the paper. Prayers for example—although fairly short—came to fruition within the pages of my journal.

As I wrangled with anger and sought after a biblical response to my feelings, I took notes in my journal. Within the privacy of my journal, the Lord answered my dilemma. Writing things down signified survival for me.

Journaling also becomes our own personal testimony of God's grace. Years later we can look back and marvel at how far we've come.

Put better days to good use.

On better-than-normal days, or during better-than-normal moments, work harder and get more done so you can afford to slack off on the worst days.

Grit your teeth, pray, take a deep breath, and just do it.

My insurance company caused me an enormous amount of frustration, requiring way too many phone calls to get them to cover our health expenses. As mentioned, after Brian's death, I continued to receive hospital bills, which should've been completely covered by insurance.

Every bill drew memories and reminders of my loss. I avoided making calls as much as possible, but some days I literally had to say a prayer, take a deep breath, and just do it. When I finally fell apart on the phone and sobbed one day, the lady on the other end found the compassion to fix the problem. Tears sometimes work in our favor!

Focus where you can when you can.

Similar to putting good days to good use, take advantage of a day in which you can focus better. Forcing yourself to focus where you can will help you focus better overall.

Reward yourself for accomplishing tough tasks.

Who doesn't like a reward? If something needs to get done but you just can't find the strength to do it, offer yourself a reward. Motivation never hurts.

Allow yourself time to cry, and then pick yourself up and get something—anything—done.

My mom gets credit for this one. She discovered if she allowed herself to cry for a certain period of time (say, thirty minutes to an hour or so), then she accomplished more afterward. Allowing a certain amount of unproductivity can actually lead to more productivity in the long run—if you manage it.

Put one foot in front of the other and drag yourself to important events.

When all else fails, and especially if your children need you to attend some event, you must drag yourself there whether or not you feel like it. At times my legs literally felt like lead. Just walking seemed like an impossible task. Do not allow yourself to skip out on important activities for your kids. They've already lost one parent. They need you to show up—if only in body.

SLEEP

Even months after Brian's death, my evenings stretched into the stillness of early morning without my notice. I looked for new ways to avoid the cavernous bed until my tiny frame collapsed into it. I stayed up way too late hoping to avoid the pain associated with my half-empty bed, thinking the later I collapsed into it, the easier sleep might come. When I finally gave in to the night, I laid lengthwise across the bed in an effort to alleviate the terrible emptiness.

I quickly became a statistic in the sleep department. While grief and depression cause some to sleep too much, I landed into the category of those who sleep too little. Like many widows, and those suffering grief, I found it impossible to achieve a healthy sleep pattern.

One medication I tried knocked me out, but I woke up four hours later, unable to sleep more. My doctor finally recommended a blood pressure medication that shut off my thoughts, allowing better rest.

Sleep never came easily for me, and the stress of loss made it even harder. My children also battled falling and staying asleep, which made everyday life in our home extremely complex.

Though they suffered from sleep deprivation and an inability to focus, my kids had no choice but to continue with school. They managed to hang on and pretend throughout the school day, but homework turned into a daily disaster as they lost the ability to keep pushing at home. This melded into late nights.

Some nights, the kids came into my room crying, unable to sleep because they missed their dad, and the pressures of school compounded their angst. At times we had to forego homework and cry. Other times they fell asleep in my bed with homework on their laps. Grades plummeted for two out of the three.

Doctors don't hand prescriptions for sleeping medication to children as readily as they do to adults. The pediatrician did finally prescribe medication for one of my kids for a time. We also tried Benadryl but didn't always obtain relief. Lack of sleep compounds the brutality of grief.

Symptoms

According to the American Academy of Sleep Medicine, the "effects of sleep deprivation are widespread" and include the following: irritability, lack of motivation, anxiety, depression, lack of concentration, attention deficits, reduced vigilance, longer reaction times, distractibility, lack of energy, fatigue, restlessness, lack of coordination, poor decisions, increased errors, forgetfulness, high blood pressure, heart attack, obesity, and diabetes.[5]

Wow! As if we need *more* problems.

Cures

Our bodies crave sleep. They also scream at us when we get too little of it by manifesting any number of the above symptoms. The cure? Like everything else, solutions abound, but the power of grief sometimes overpowers even the best ones.

Obviously the quickest and easiest answer is medication. If sleep eludes you, don't fear taking a sleep aid. You lost your best friend. You lived through trauma, of which one of the symptoms includes the inability to sleep. As the list above states, insomnia affects our health. Ask for help. Talk to your doctor.

After her son was killed in Afghanistan, Shelley didn't sleep for months. Her husband begged her to get help. Sandra tried numerous medications with no results after her daughter died suddenly without explanation. She constantly asked her friends what medications they took because she couldn't find one that worked for her. See also the book section "Prayer and Medication."

Other possible help may come in the form of exercise, relaxation techniques such as biofeedback, and natural remedies. Talk to your doctor or pharmacist to make sure no possible drug interactions exist before trying natural products recommended for sleep.

I tried natural remedies, but it took the blood pressure medication to help me achieve the most rest. In addition to antidepressants, exercise helped my outlook. Sometimes we need to ask for help in order to function for a while. That's okay.

FORGETTING

"And suddenly at the very moment when, so far, I mourned [Joy] least, I remembered her best."

~ C.S. Lewis, A Grief Observed

At some point we begin to forget. One day I tried to remember what Brian wore to bed at night. For the life of me, I couldn't remember. Of course, it doesn't really matter what he wore to bed at night, but the fact that I forgot upset me greatly.

Guilt

Interestingly, we tend to feel guilty when we forget even small, unimportant things. I don't know why we think we should remember everything in the first place. Perhaps we fear it means we don't love our lost spouse anymore if we forget. The truth is, we would forget certain things even if they still lived. So what makes their death any different? Maybe because we don't *want* to forget. We cling to memories because that's all we have left.

Just as we do with regret, we need to forgive ourselves for our humanity and our inability to remember everything. As the years pass, Brian no longer graces my daily presence, and I will forget little things. I can write them down if it means that much, but I also need to remind myself that Brian stands in the presence of Jesus now. He doesn't really care if I remember what he wore to bed.

Children also grieve their forgotten memories. My daughter cried because she couldn't remember what her dad looked like anymore. Of course we brought out pictures, but she wanted to remember his laugh, what it felt like to be swooped up in his arms, and what kind of advice he would give when she dates her first boyfriend. I can tell her what he would've said. I can share my journals with her that tell our story, but nothing replaces his presence. I asked the kids one day what they missed most about their dad. Nikki profoundly summed it up, "Him."

Healthy Memory Loss

Some things fit the category of healthy memory loss, especially if we remarry. I don't want to forget Brian or all the wonderful memories and years we shared. When I chose to remarry, however, I chose to not dwell on certain parts of my memory. It's not that I can't still recall some of those memories, but I choose to put my focus elsewhere.

When I found myself forced into widowhood, I enjoyed all of my memories, and I think they all qualified as healthy. But when we married, Howard and I both specifically chose *not* to dwell on memories of our sex lives with our first spouse. In this instance, we needed to create our own, new memories. This doesn't mean we never remember sex with our first spouse, but we choose to focus on memories from our current marriage.

Memories of different sorts should fit into different categories. If dwelling on any sort of memory gets in the way of a current marriage, maybe we should rethink it. Memories alone can't hurt, but dwelling too much on certain kinds of memories can bring pain and hurt to other relationships.

Balance

Overall, we need to balance our memories. Remember the good times. Forgive the bad. Realize some memories will fall by the wayside, and others will etch themselves forever in our minds. Some of them should not monopolize our thoughts. Hopefully somewhere along the line, we will find balance.

PRAYER AND MEDICATION

"I cannot deny the validity of prayer or the reality of God."

~James Means

"Prayer became not only a holy endeavor, but also a necessary ingredient."

~Lois Mowday Rabey

"Prayer is no guarantee against trouble, but it is a guarantee against defeat."

~Calvin O. Butts, III

"I just don't know how you do it, Fran," my neighbor exclaimed. "Lots of prayer and medication," I shot back.

I willingly admit to taking medication for sleep, as well as to help cope emotionally. But prayer played a vital role.

Prayer

During the fight for Brian's life, George inquired about Brian and quickly stopped himself. He rephrased the question. "No. How are *you* doing?"

I honestly shared how some days I survived by God's grace alone. George vowed to pray for me every day that week. I reminded myself daily of George's pledge to pray. The knowledge alone, of someone else in prayer on my behalf, gave me strength to keep trudging. Even now, years later, George continues to pray for me, as well as for my new family.

I cannot express how much it means to hear people continually say they pray regularly for me and my family. Nancy prays through two prayer journals daily. I meet her for lunch once or twice a year to catch her up on our lives because she prays for every member of my family every day.

Gloria, a beautiful elderly lady bent over with osteoporosis, asks specific questions about our ministry and family. She ministers to me on a regular basis through her interest, compassion, and commitment to prayer.

These friends don't typify the "norm," but we all need people in our lives committed to praying us through. I know for sure I progressed this far because of the many who pray for me regularly.

Antidepressants

I lost all desire to move forward in life. I forced myself out of bed to take the children to school and often crawled back in when I returned home. I lacked the energy to cook or clean, and I wanted to hide from everyone. I cried all the time, feeling completely alone, abandoned, and incapable of pressing onward.

I realized my kids needed more of me than I could give. They desired and required a fully functioning parent. I needed help to truly be present. My kids deserved better. Their emotional health depended on mine.

I asked for help. I told my doctor I lacked motivation, desire, and energy. She changed my medication. I found a counselor, started making strategic decisions to improve my outlook, and slowly I came back to life.

Don't be too proud to admit you need help and to ask for it. When you accept help, you not only give a gift to yourself but also to others around you. Mixing medication (as directed by your doctor) with prayer can salve the wound and assist the healing process.

Antidepressants don't necessarily numb emotions, although some can. Believe me, I still experienced pain and lots of emotion, but I no longer cried all the time. Antidepressants take the edge off the worst of your pain so you can function in daily life.

As I mention in the "Depression" section, we take medications for all kinds of physical ailments, but for some reason we try to "tough it out" when it comes to our emotional well-being. If we don't take care of ourselves emotionally, we also risk our physical well-being. Should you experience negative side effects, your doctor can prescribe something else. Communicate closely with your doctor.

According to WebMD.com, "Grief can cause prolonged and serious symptoms, including depression, anxiety, suicidal thoughts and actions, physical illness, and post-traumatic stress disorder."[6] This list represents proven side effects to grief. We could probably label grief as an illness, since it slaps us in the face and sucks us down like quicksand.

Obviously you should talk to your doctor to determine whether or not you need medication, and if so, which kind. Many people believe taking medication makes them weak or ungodly. But I want to encourage you to get help if you need it. Asking for help actually proves strength.

Side Effects

Many different options of medications exist. Discuss them with your doctor. Unfortunately, side effects can occur with antidepressants. If you experience negative side effects, let your doctor know. And never quit taking antidepressants suddenly, unless advised by your physician to do so. You will likely spiral downward quickly if you do. I learned this the hard way.

A common side effect to antidepressants is loss of libido. This may actually come as a welcome relief—instead of a problem—at this stage of your life.

Sleep Aids

Many sleep aids are available. Again, talk to your doctor about what might work for you if you experience trouble sleeping (insomnia). Some medications help you go to sleep, but don't help you stay asleep. Others help calm your mind when you can't stop thinking or reliving painful memories.

As you probably know, numerous natural products can also help. Consider these a temporary fix. None of these medications are intended for long-term use, but they may help you get some sleep during the worst of your grief by forcing rest when you need it most.

As mentioned before, my friend Shelley slept only about two hours a night for months after her son died in Afghanistan. Her husband finally insisted she get help when her inability to sleep began affecting others around her. Please don't allow yourself to go that long without assistance.

Anxiety Meds

Loss of a loved one can cause anxiety and fear. Sometimes we must allow ourselves the luxury of taking medication for a period of time. Understand that it takes courage to request help when you need it. If you feel embarrassed about taking medication, keep the information to yourself. No one else really needs to know.

Again, your doctor must determine the right medications and monitor your progress, as side effects may occur. Honestly discuss with your doctor your feelings about, and experience with, the medications you take.

Medication Abuse

We've all been there. The thought crosses our minds. What a wonderful thought to not have to wake up tomorrow. *Do not go there.*

Please don't abuse medications. Prescription abuse will cause more pain for yourself and your family. Temptation to abuse medications in your worst moments is common. Acting on it fixes nothing. If you can't shake the temptation, get help immediately! Please don't do anything that causes more pain for your loved ones.

TAKE CARE OF YOURSELF

"Don't depend on others to give you permission to grieve—give that permission to yourself."

~Kenneth Haugk

"Take care of yourself!" or "Well, you *look* great!" people often exclaim when ending a conversation, as if their casual utterance fixes everything.

I think our friends who compliment us after a difficult conversation lack the ability to end the dialogue on a painful note. They feel the need to say something positive. While there's nothing wrong with flattery, it doesn't meet the need we crave in our souls to be heard and understood.

Realistically, these kinds of statements simply allow a person to end the conversation, albeit in an awkward manner, leaving a widow feeling alone and discouraged.

Although these friends may not know the best time to throw out clumsy statements, they do make an important point. We should take care of ourselves as much as possible.

Appearance

My standard advice to those who hurt: "You gotta do what you gotta do." Yes, for a time, go easy on yourself. Eventually, though, too much slack becomes damaging. At some point we must begin to force ourselves to make healthy choices—both emotionally and physically, but at the beginning, we strive only for survival.

Here's my honest confession: For a long time after Brian died, I quit washing my face at night. I lived in a state of exhaustion, and washing my face each night took too much effort. Also, I often skipped brushing my teeth before going to bed. Who cared or would even notice anyway? (I did always brush them in the morning). Clearly not the healthiest choice. But in my survival mentality, I needed to allow myself some slack until coping came easier.

I cut myself some slack when I stayed at home. I didn't bother with makeup. If I went to church or to a function for one of the kids at school, I put on make-up, fixed my hair and dressed nicely. When we fix ourselves up, especially before we go out in public, we naturally feel better about ourselves. At least we look half decent, and people won't talk about how bad we look. An old saying goes, "Fake it 'til you make it." In one sense, dressing respectably and making some effort with our appearance achieves this.

I learned that putting forth some effort when it came to my appearance also helped me emotionally and psychologically. A number of months after Brian died, I decided to get a makeover. It was a little drastic and some of my friends raved over how good I looked. My response to them: "This is my 'let's pretend Fran is doing well when she's actually doing lousy' look."

Food

I watch widows and widowers regularly fall into the food trap. Most either gain or lose too much weight. Few maintain their normal, healthy weight. Grief greatly affects our eating habits.

Definitely give yourself a break at times, and don't worry about cooking. If at all possible, try to eat nutritional meals and snacks most of the time. Poor eating habits will affect how you feel physically and can contribute to a downward spiral emotionally, as well as giving you a poor self-image.

Emotional eaters battle with weight gain more than others. Force yourself to find some form of balance. If you allow yourself to put on too much weight, you will hate yourself for it eventually. Plus you face the stress of trying to lose it. Remind yourself that your spouse wouldn't want you to let yourself go completely.

I fit into the category of those who lose too much weight. I felt nauseated for eight months after Brian died. I found it took too much effort to eat. I ate mostly soup and food that slid down easily. I drank the highest-calorie chocolate Ensure every night before going to bed to avoid losing more weight.

Dietitians will tell you to eat every three to four hours even if you don't feel hungry. Cheese and crackers, a protein bar, a high protein shake or a drink like Ensure or Boost will help sustain some energy and weight.

This is one of those really tough things to balance. On the one hand, I would say, do what you have to do to survive. On the other hand, your health depends on your eating habits. Try to balance the scales to the best of your ability, without gaining or losing too much weight.

Apparently the experience of grief creates an enzyme that tends to dehydrate our bodies and affect our thinking. "Some studies suggest increasing the amount of water you drink can help flush the [grief] enzyme out of your system and give some relief."[7]

Exercise

I know you don't want to hear this. It's challenging to incorporate exercise into our routines when we're doing well emotionally, and even more difficult when we're depressed. But it's one of the best things we can do for ourselves. Exercise releases endorphins that help emotions. I recommend finding a friend willing to walk or work out with you, or hire a trainer if you can afford it. Set a regular schedule and stick to it.

I began by meeting my friend Susan at the mall once a week to walk, and eventually added a simple exercise program for the rest of the week. We pounded the floor with our feet while we poured out our hearts. I started looking forward to our Friday morning therapy sessions, and slowly joy crept back into my life. I can't tell you enough how much exercise helped me emotionally. Doctors agree that exercise is essential to our emotional well-being.

Honor

Honor the wishes of your love by taking care of yourself as well as you can. Most spouses would not want us to "go to pot," so to speak. Reminding ourselves of what they would want sometimes helps motivate us to take good care of our physical body and keep trudging on.

Emotional

Part of taking care of yourself includes being proactive with regard to your emotional needs. This may involve sharing your needs with others, seeing a counselor, going to a GriefShare group, finding a trusted friend with whom you can talk openly, joining a widow's group, and/or taking medication to take the edge off the searing pain.

Standing up for your needs and kindly teaching others what that looks like to you also qualifies as taking care of your emotional needs. Dixie's friend totally wore her out with constant questions. Instead of encouraging Dixie, the friend drained her emotionally. Dixie finally wrote the following and gave it to her friend the next day.

> "Ask me no questions, dear friend unless you have walked my way. Tell me your joys and your sorrows. Give me a hug; Tell me you love me, then gently walk away. My friend understood," she wrote, "hugged me, told me she loved me and gently walked away."[8]

Early on, I also tired of answering too many questions, or telling my story over and over again. After a while, I didn't mind the questions, for the most part, because I wanted people to understand. As long as they listened with compassion, I willingly shared my heart, especially to my close friends. Be honest with your friends about your needs.

Spiritual

The Bible says, "The widow who is really in need and left all alone puts her hope in God and continues night and day to pray and to ask God for help." (1 Tim. 5:5). In my opinion, hope does not exist without God. This verse says the widow puts all of her hope in God and continues to plead with him for help. Sometimes that's all we can manage for a while.

TRUST

"Each crisis presents me with the opportunity for a stretching, growing, God-honoring act of resolute trust."

~James Means

"Who can you trust?" June asked me. That's a very good question, and a difficult one to answer.

Family

Some of us can't trust family. Some can. Usually, certain family members deserve our trust, while others don't. Likely, you had already figured out on whom you could rely while your spouse was still alive. But often a death in the family can cause relationship twists, and we realize—somewhat unexpectedly—that circumstances changed when we most needed them to stay the same. Now, for some reason, those we thought we could depend on turn on us, and we can no longer trust them.

This scenario plays out in more stories than I can count. Sometimes it's about money. Sometimes differences in needs or expressions of grief bring on the changes. Often a family will turn against the person who made the decision either to remove life support or not to resuscitate. Whatever your story, it hurts.

Janis's step-son went through her things—drawers, closets, cabinets, garage—after his dad died. The step-son feared she would hide something he deemed his own. He failed to realize his step-mom's home didn't belong to him, and he didn't own rights to its contents. He, a counselor by trade, failed to see how his behavior insulted his already distraught step-mother.

June nursed her husband for five years while he battled brain cancer. After one resuscitation, she decided it would be cruel and unfair to force another. She prevented the next resuscitation, and he died. Almost two years later, her grown daughter won't speak to her. She cannot recognize that her mother acted out of love and compassion for her husband, who suffered greatly.

Unfortunately, we can't change the minds of those who turn on us. We can, however, set boundaries to prevent more pain and hurt. I feel strongly that we must stand up for our own needs, but we can do it in a kind manner. See also "In-Laws" and "Relationships."

Friends

Sadly, the friend situation models that of families. When death occurs, friendships change, and we can't always trust the same people we trusted in the past. June can't seem to rely on anyone. Her pain runs so deep that her friends cannot comprehend her needs, so they ignore her. She feels completely alone even among so-called friends, and her feelings of aloneness intensify her depression. On the brink of suicide, she reached out to me for help. She literally didn't know whom she could trust.

June needs new friends, but she lacks the strength to search. In her despair, she can't afford the effort to risk trusting anyone, including her pastor.

I encouraged her to find a GriefShare class somewhere. I thought maybe she could meet some people who understand loss, and gain encouragement from that connection. I also offered to meet with her. She can trust me, though I doubt she fully believes that.

Friend, if you find yourself in this situation, you probably need some medical and professional help. Many churches offer GriefShare classes. It takes some effort and guts to walk through the door for the first time (or the 20th). But everyone in attendance shares the experience of loss, which means you're not alone.

Most churches can also either provide counseling or point you to someone who can help. Please don't allow yourself to continue in a downward spiral of depression without getting help. See also "Prayer and Medication," and "Depression."

God

I know a lot of people feel they can't even trust God. They think he let them down. Many wonder how a good God could let someone die—especially a child, or a young parent with children who need them. I understand the confusion. It certainly feels that way at times.

If we can't trust God himself, whom *can* we trust? I find it interesting that when good things happen, we tend to either feel we don't need God or we talk about how good he is. When bad things happen to other people, we tell them to "Just trust God." But when bad things happen to us, we often assume he abandoned us.

We must decide which theology to follow. If we believe God is good in good times, why would our beliefs change in bad times? I don't understand everything God does or everything he allows, but I consider Him my only hope. If I didn't have God to hang on to, I would continually find myself in a much darker place. Scripture addresses my fears and gives me courage to keep going, even one more day.

If you would like to read more on this topic, I recommend the following:

- *A Grace Disguised* by Jerry Sittser
- *A Tearful Celebration* by James Means
- *Reflections of a Grieving Spouse* by H. Norman Wright
- *Honest Wrestling*[9] by K. Howard Joslin

Praise be to the Lord, for he has *heard* my cry for *mercy*. The *Lord* is my *strength* and My *shield*. My heart *trusts* in him And *I am healed*.

Psalm 28:6–7

Better is one day in your courts than a thousand elsewhere. . . . For the Lord God is a *sun* and *shield*; the Lord bestows *favor* and *honor*; no *good thing* does he withhold from those whose walk is blameless. O Lord Almighty, *blessed* is the man who *trusts* in you.

Psalm 84:10a; 11–12

(emphasis mine, from my journal)

Section Three

MANY EMOTIONS

ANGER

"I see now that my faith was becoming an ally rather than an enemy because I could vent anger freely, even toward God, without fearing retribution."

~ Jerry Sittser, A Grace Disguised

I admit it. I raged with anger. I wanted to believe I expressed "righteous anger," of course. Whatever it was, my friends and family listened to me rant over and over again. I didn't deserve this situation. Others couldn't seem to express love to me properly. People judged and criticized me and my kids in our hour of greatest need. Weariness sucked me into quicksand. I bore the burden of parenting my kids completely alone. The list went on. I spent a lot of time thinking and praying about my anger, wondering where the line crossed from normal, righteous anger to sin.

Normal Anger

Although extremely frustrating at times, anger naturally accompanies grief. The simple fact that we feel anger can make us angry. Many of us who grieve actually get angry with the deceased for leaving us, even if we know they didn't choose to die.

Anger toward God commonly happens, as well as anger toward anyone who treats us poorly. Those who faced a difficult marriage or "unfinished business" with their spouse also feel angry that closure didn't occur.

In the event of a suicide, even if mental illness exists, intense anger can consume us.

What the Bible says about anger:

1. God's character: slow to anger

If I want to follow him, I should also want to emulate his qualities. The hard part? As humans, we fail. As widows, we brawl more than ever with out-of-control emotions. Widowed humans make for quite a difficult mix.

Plead with God to guide you in your anger. Our *goal* should be to live lives that are compassionate, gracious, slow-to-anger, and abounding-in-love. On this side of heaven, none of us will fully accomplish this goal. Even in our grief, though, we should continue to strive, with God's help, to walk with God and manage our anger in a godly way.

- "The Lord, the Lord, the compassionate and gracious God, slow to anger, abounding in love and faithfulness" (Ex. 34:6).
- "The Lord is slow to anger, abounding in love and forgiving sin and rebellion" (Num. 14:18).
- "But you, O Lord, are a compassionate God, slow to anger, abounding in love and faithfulness" (Psalm 86:15).
- "The Lord is compassionate and gracious; slow to anger, abounding in love" (Psalm 103:8).
- "I knew that you are a gracious and compassionate God, slow to anger and abounding in love" (Jonah 4:2).

2. God's Character: just

We need to let God deal with difficult people, as well as with things that hurt us or make us angry. Constantly commit your anger to the Lord because he can handle it. Take comfort in the fact that God will deal with others in his own time and in his own way. This, in no way, takes away the anger. It simply puts it in God's hands.

- In both the Exodus and Numbers passages listed above, the phrase ends by saying, "*Yet* he does not leave the guilty unpunished" (emphasis mine).
- "Do not take revenge, my friends, but leave room for God's wrath, for it is written, 'It is mine to avenge; I will repay,' says the Lord" (Rom. 12:19).
- "Do not take advantage of a widow *or* an orphan. If you do and they cry out to me, I *will* certainly *hear* their cry. My anger will be aroused, and I will kill you with the sword; your wives will become widows and your children fatherless" (Ex. 22:22–24, emphasis mine).

I love this last verse. Not because I want to see anyone hurt, but because God is serious about protecting widows and orphans. He will deal with those who push us to cry out to him. I find so much comfort in knowing that fact.

3. Be angry but do not sin.

Scripture clearly states that anger is not inherently wrong. Go ahead. Get angry. Express your anger. The challenge? Voicing anger without sin.

- "In your anger do not sin: Do not let the sun go down while you are still angry, and do not let the devil get a foothold" (Eph. 4:26–27).

- "Everyone should be quick to listen, slow to speak and slow to become angry, for man's anger does not bring about the righteous life that God desires" (James 1:19–20).

We manage to avoid sinning in anger when we don't let the sun go down while angry and when we keep the devil under control. This means we deal with our anger and don't dwell on it. The more we dwell on it, the bigger it gets.

Yes. Dealing with anger is excruciatingly difficult. I really think the key in managing our anger lies in constantly taking our pain and anger to the Lord. Fill journals with feelings; talk to trusted and safe friends; try to talk out problems with a counselor if possible. Not everyone willingly works through differences with us, though, and the rejection can bring more anger and frustration.

Believe me, I do not want to downplay the difficulties because I understand. We must hold ourselves accountable to a standard of godliness even in our anger and hurt, though, because "anger does not bring about the righteous life that God desires" (James 1:20).

4. Jesus expressed anger.

Jesus got so angry—on the Sabbath, no less—that he turned over tables in the synagogue. This knowledge challenges our thinking. We usually discipline children for throwing things (like toys or rocks), and rightly so. Can you imagine if your child turned over one of your tables in a fit of anger? Children and teens don't usually show anger for righteous reasons, though, and in our culture, we would likely discipline them for throwing things out of *any* kind of anger.

I cannot easily dictate how you should behave when you're angry. However, I can tell you what the Bible says and encourage you to follow God's wisdom even when it feels unbearable.

We will certainly not always master our anger. We will not always face anger for righteous reasons. And we cannot help the fact that we feel anger.

I do not know how to encourage you if you don't personally know the Lord Jesus himself. In my experience, the only option is to cling to the Lord in humility, plead with him for victory over anger, and ask for his strength to act righteously.

And let me encourage you that anger *does* eventually soften as we walk through grief and cling to the Lord.

Blessed are those who mourn, for they *will be* comforted.

Matthew 5:4
(emphasis mine from my journal)

DEPRESSION

"Grief is like sinking, like being buried. I am in water the tawny color of kicked up dirt. Every breath is full of choking. There is nothing to hold on to, no sides, no way to claw myself up."

~ Lauren Oliver, Pandemonium

"Without you in my arms, I feel an emptiness in my soul. I find myself searching the crowds for your face."

~ Nicholas Sparks, Message in a Bottle

"I am deeply hurt and hurting deeply!" read my journal entry seven months after Brian died. And as time passed: "I feel like I'm not a good parent. I miss Brian so badly. I stay up too late in order to fall asleep quickly. I cry so much. I don't want to cook. Someone else's engagement upset me deeply. I don't want to clean the house, do dishes, make phone calls, etc."

And, to top it off, I felt guilty about all of it. My doctor's diagnosis: depression.

Overwhelmed

Good grief! Who *wouldn't* be depressed?

I once told my friend, Barbara, "I feel overwhelmed."

She wisely countered, "That's because you *are* overwhelmed." She listed numerous difficulties I faced and finished by stating, "It's a miracle that you function at all." Oh! How dumb of me not to realize it. Of course she was completely right, but I judged myself for my failure to cope well.

Clinical Depression

Grief, stress, long term illness, and the like can actually alter hormones, causing a chemical imbalance in the brain, and therefore, clinical depression. Many people feel they should just tough it out because they shouldn't take medication. They think taking antidepressants shows weakness.

Christians often feel they just need to trust the Lord. "I want to say this once and for all. Christians get depressed—sometimes very depressed," said Leslie Vernick, a licensed Christian counselor.[10]

Absolutely, we must trust the Lord. But, if you break your foot, you don't tell the doctor you just need to tough it out and trust the Lord. You allow the doctor to put a cast on it, or you wear a boot so it can heal.

Taking antidepressants should be no different. They are a wonderful invention that can help take the edge off your pain in order to help you cope and heal. See also also "Prayer and Medication." If you feel deeply depressed, ask your doctor if you need help in the form of medication.

Mild Depression

Obviously, mild depression affects us in a less oppressive way than clinical depression, but we ought not to ignore it. The list below helps most forms of mild depression:

- Exercise (there's that word again) is the single best thing you can do for depression. Exercise releases endorphins that help depression.

- Take intentional and purposeful steps to do things that you enjoy. Get out of the house and walk briskly for fifteen minutes, go shopping, have dinner with a trusted friend, or whatever brings you joy. Granted, you will likely not enjoy anything as much at this point as you used to, but keep trying. It *will* get easier.

- Do something you've always wanted to do—take a dance class, a home improvement class, join a book club, or something else you find enjoyable.

- Find activities that make you laugh. Laughing also releases endorphins, and it's just plain fun. Watch funny movies or spend time with someone who makes you laugh. Laughter brings enormous relief from our pain.

- Read through the Psalms. The Psalms are full of joy, as well as pain and lament. I found lots of encouragement from seeing that the psalmist himself suffered from depression. He freely expressed his pain and continually cried out for God's mercy.

Some of our friends enjoyed Irish line dancing. We gathered a group of all ages, including families, and learned to dance. Along with antidepressants, the dancing parties became part of the healing process for me.

Honestly, I'm not sure I could've forced myself to find fun activities without the help of the antidepressants.

My flesh and my heart may fail, but God is the strength of my heart and my portion forever.

Psalm 73:26

The Lord is close to the brokenhearted, and saves those who are crushed in spirit.

Psalm 34:18

He heals the brokenhearted and binds up their wounds.

Psalm 147:3

LONELINESS

"But grief is a walk alone. Others can be there, and listen. But you will walk alone down your own path, at your own pace, with your sheared-off pain, your raw wounds, your denial, anger, and bitter loss. You'll come to your own peace, hopefully, but it will be on your own, in your own time."

~ Cathy Lamb, *The First Day of the Rest of My Life*

Eighty percent of the widows and widowers who responded to my survey listed loneliness as the hardest thing they face. Loneliness can drag us down emotionally.

Journal Entries

Following are some excerpts from my journal written the first year after Brian's death.

- Again tonight I feel weak and shaky like I did that first week. I feel so alone and broken! Aug. 27, 2008

- I mindlessly flip channels on the TV like I did during the early days after Brian's first diagnosis. I'm so lonely without my love! Jan. 11, 2009

- I think reality has hit! Jan asked if my heart is beginning to heal. I really feel like the hole gapes wider—maybe there's infection now. I feel completely alone. I realize how often I went to Brian for reinforcement, direction (at least discussion), and for emotional support. He was so gracious to always be there for me. I know the Lord is there for me, but he doesn't give physical hugs, and I would give almost anything right now for one big hug from Brian. Jan. 21, 2009

- I feel completely alone in this world! I appreciate my friends so much, but no one is Brian, and I feel so much like I need him with all that happened lately! Aug. 28, 2009

- I feel like I'm on a downward spiral because even though I have great friends, I still feel *all alone!* Aug. 30, 2009

Completely Alone

It amazes me how much support we can receive from family and friends and yet still feel completely alone. Typically, we talk to our friends and family members during the day. We talk to them briefly, though, and then we're alone again.

After a lunch date we go home alone. After church we return to an empty house. Even after grocery shopping, going home leaves us alone. Our best friend and partner no longer rejoins us at home, and no form of communication reaches him in heaven. We feel completely and utterly alone.

Alone in a Crowd

Going out can leave us feeling alone as well. If we go out with couples, we feel alone. We feel alone in a crowd at church because even if we sit with a friend or with our children, our spouse doesn't sit with us anymore.

Bill expressed how much he feels alone, even when he's with other family members. Couples make a unit. When one member of that unit dies, we even feel alone in the middle of a crowd. Every single thing that once involved our spouse reminds us that we now exist as one, and we feel isolated, secluded, and completely void of life itself.

Missing the Negatives

Early in our marriage, Brian teased me about some silly habit. I shot back, "Hey, you would miss this if I died." How profoundly true! I now miss his silly habits. He regularly emptied his pockets on his dresser, creating dusty piles. Although I cleaned off his dresser soon after he died, I found myself dreaming again for the dusty mess because it signified his presence here with me.

Life with a cancer patient was extremely difficult, but I wished it all back just to have him near me. Sadly, no matter how much I wanted him back, he couldn't come back. Simply knowing that he couldn't return from the grave increased my loneliness. I could not comprehend how to go on in life without my best friend.

Solution

I hate it. No solution to the loneliness really exists, other than staying busy, but even then the loneliness attacks at the end of the day. The only solution I could muster was to find my comfort in the Lord.

I clung to him in my darkest hours. I cried out to him and begged him for strength to walk through the loneliness each day. I read passages from the Psalms and took note of David's loneliness. Imagine! Even king David, who had anything and everything, not to mention tons of wives, still felt alone and needed his Lord for comfort.

Keep in mind that finding comfort in God does not mean we don't feel lonely. We simply lean on the Lord through the loneliness and find comfort in the fact that, although we *feel* alone, we are *not* alone. Thankfully, when he takes away, he himself does not go away.

From my Journal Nov. 11, 2008:[11]

Better is one day in your courts than a thousand Elsewhere. . . . For the Lord God is a *sun* and *shield*; the Lord bestows *favor* and *honor*; *no good thing* does he withhold from those whose walk is blameless. O Lord Almighty, *blessed* is the man who *trusts* in You.

Psalm 84:10; 11–12

Death has been swallowed up in victory!

1 Corinthians 15:54

Even though I walk through the valley of the shadow of death . . . you are *with* me . . . [and] *comfort* me.

Psalm 23:4

Whether we live or die, we *belong* to the Lord.

Romans 14:8

Blessed are the dead who die in the Lord. . . . They will rest from their labor.

Revelation 14:13

I *feel* all alone, but I *am not!*

SUDDEN MELTDOWNS

"And like lava surging to the surface of a mountainous volcano, sobs and tears erupted and wouldn't stop."

~ H. Norman Wright

S udden meltdowns overcome us when we least expect them. One minute we feel perfectly fine, and the next we dissolve into a puddle of uncontrollable sobs.

Visuals

As I entered a pharmacy seven years after my dad's death, the Valentine's visuals hit me and stirred the same emotions I experienced that Valentine's morning when I ran into the hospital knowing my dad would die that day.

This time, I ran into the pharmacy to purchase something for someone else, and suddenly I found myself reeling from the pain of my loss seven years earlier. I managed to pick out a gift for my friend and also selected a rose to put on Brian's grave. But then, as I made my purchase at the counter, the tears began. One would think after seven years you could contain your emotions in public. Not so!

Surprises

I went to see my Ob-gyn for my yearly appointment. For the first time ever, I circled the word "widow." The nurse then asked what kind of birth control I use. Uh, that would be called "death." I cried through the entire appointment.

Thankfully my doctor knew me well. He treated me with gentleness and loving-kindness and graciously apologized for the nurse's ignorant question. He ended the appointment appropriately, "Well, you look great, even though you feel like hell." He got it.

Memories

I play hand bells. When we performed at church, I could always see Brian out of the corner of my right eye. While we practiced one night after his death, a picture of

Brian flashed to my right out of nowhere. A waterfall spilled out. I blinked repeatedly in an effort to read my music as I tried to finish the piece. Others in the group peered at me as if to ask, "What on earth happened to you?"

Alone

The night our church celebrated the retirement of their pastor—my father-in-law—I behaved as if I were attending a funeral instead of a retirement party. This event, the first gathering of the entire family since Brian's death about a year prior, brought the ache in my heart to an unbearable level.

One of the leaders of the church began introducing the pastor's children, all of whom attended except Brian. I don't know what I expected, but I was completely unprepared when the leader asked my kids and me to stand and then introduced us to the crowd as "Brian's family." Exposed, vulnerable, and feeling completely alone, I sobbed as if Brian died just yesterday. I stayed for the party as long as I could manage, apologized for my behavior and drove home, humiliated and fearful that people might judge me as "making it all about her."

In the least, it would've helped me to know ahead of time that family introductions would be made and we would be asked to stand. Sadness and loneliness conquered me before the service even began. The introductions threw me off guard, and I could no longer contain the tears I had tried so hard to hold back.

How Long?

I could continue with many more stories just like these, but you get the picture. The reality is, I can actually talk about my loss without tears—quite often. As the years pass the meltdowns lessen, but I'm not sure how long they will lurk, ready to pounce at any moment.

I still cry when I meet someone who discloses her status of widow. I grieve for our children who continue to feel a void and experience painful reminders and ramifications of their losses. I go to the cemetery on my anniversary or on Father's Day and cry in Howard's arms over Brian's absence.

Sudden meltdowns happen—for how long they will keep happening, I don't know. I'm sure it varies with everyone. We feel stupid, but we can't help ourselves. We cannot contain the sickness of grief. While at times it appears dormant, like an angry volcano, grief erupts at any given moment.

My advice? Just go with it. We can't just turn off the spigot of tears. Sudden meltdowns are completely normal, and we don't need to apologize for them. Our tears testify to the love we shared with our spouse. Feel free to explain your breakdowns, but don't fall into the trap of feeling the need to apologize for them.

Eventually we somehow learn to live with—and embrace—the dichotomy of joy and sorrow.

LORD, HELP ME!

"Leave it all in the Hands that were wounded for you."

~ Elizabeth Elliot, *Keep a Quiet Heart*

Clinging to the Lord in my despair saved me, even though I found it difficult to focus in the midst of my intense grief. God remained my only hope.

Source of Comfort

I tried to pray, yet found it virtually impossible to complete a prayer. I pleaded with the Lord to help me pray because I needed it so badly. A full year went by before I could pray more than a sentence or two at a time. I tried to read scripture but found it hard to focus on what it said.

Strangely, I could read grief books, likely because I desperately desired a quick fix to this pain. Focusing on scripture, however, proved difficult. I recently visited a widow who finds it difficult to focus on anything but scripture. Clearly, we all react differently.

In an effort to make it easier for you, throughout this book I use scripture that encouraged me. My first advice: a fixed amount of scripture to read or time spent in prayer is not the goal. Finding your comfort in the Lord rather than other things should be the priority. After all, Jesus himself lived as "a man of sorrows, and familiar with suffering" (Isa. 53:3).

The apostle Paul wrote, "The widow who is really in need and left all alone puts her hope in God and continues night and day to pray and to ask God for help. But the widow who lives for pleasure is dead even while she lives" (1 Tim. 5:5–6).

Journal

It helps to write down what you feel. I experienced much frustration, and even guilt, over the fact that I couldn't seem to pray. Yet when I look back through my journals, I found that I regularly prayed in written form. I wrote short pleas to my Lord for help and comfort. Don't waste your energy or worries on how you pray or the length of the prayer. Simply connect with the "Father of compassion and the God of all comfort" (2 Cor. 1:3) in whatever way you can.

Short prayers fill my journal: "Lord, help me. Lord, I need your help. Lord, give us strength. Lord, give me wisdom with these kids. Calm my heart and help me to leave all my burdens with you. May I find new mercies in the morning? Oh, Lord, I need *help* and *guidance* and *wisdom*. I need sleep, wisdom, direction with rules and discipline. I need grace at the right times. Lord, I commit this day to you."

Holy Spirit

I found encouragement in the fact that certain passages of scripture came alive when experiencing them. For example, "The Spirit helps us in our weakness. We do not know what we ought to pray for, but the *Spirit himself intercedes* for us with groans that words cannot express" (Rom. 8:26, emphasis mine).

This verse came alive to me the day Brian received his cancer diagnosis. For the first time in my life, I could not find words to express my deepest need. At times after he died, I simply thanked God for the Spirit who prays on my behalf and left it at that. God knows our needs even when we can't express them. What a wonderful blessing!

Psalms

The Psalms are packed with words of encouragement, as the psalmist pours his heart out to his Lord. Consider picking a short Psalm for each day. If you can't focus even on a short passage of scripture, copy it into your journal or onto a piece of paper. By rewriting it, you may find it easier to "hear" it and therefore find comfort in it.

Word Searches

Use the concordance in your Bible to look up verses on words like "comfort," "widows," or "grief" and write them down. Biblegateway.com can help if you prefer online searches.

I searched for passages on widows and orphans and shared them with my kids. I wanted to show them that God cares about their loss and promises to take care of them. The kids reacted in amazement and felt comforted. I will save you the trouble of looking those verses up and share some of them with you here:

> Do not take advantage of a widow *or* an orphan. If you do and they cry
> out to me, I will certainly hear their cry. My anger will be aroused, and

I will kill you with the sword; your wives will become widows and your children fatherless.

Exodus 22:22–24 (emphasis mine)

For the Lord your God is God of gods and Lord of Lords, the great God, mighty and awesome, who shows no partiality and accepts no bribes. He defends the cause of the fatherless and the widow, and loves the alien, giving him food and clothing.

Deuteronomy 10:17–18

Sing to the Lord, sing praise to his name, extol him who rides on the clouds—his name is the Lord—and rejoice before him. A father to the fatherless, a defender of widows, is God in his holy dwelling.

Psalm 68:4–5

Learn to do right! Seek justice, encourage the oppressed. Defend the cause of the fatherless, plead the case of the widow.

Isaiah 1:17

Religion that God our Father accepts as pure and faultless is this: to look after orphans and widows in their distress and to keep oneself from being polluted by the world.

James 1:27

Give proper recognition to those widows who are really in need. But if a widow has children or grandchildren these should learn first of all to put their religion into practice by caring for their own family and so repaying their parents and grandparents, for this is pleasing to God. The widow who is really in need and left all alone puts her hope in God and continues night and day to pray and to ask God for help. But the widow who lives for pleasure is dead even while she lives.

1 Timothy 5:3–8

Excerpts from My Journal

The Lord gives and the Lord takes away. Blessed be the name of the Lord" (Job 1:21). Thankfully, when he takes away, he doesn't go away.

Elohim—God is *powerful*; the *strong* and *faithful one* . . . both to the Israelites in the past and to us in the present. Thank you, Lord, for being Elohim, the *strong* and *faithful one*, as well as Emmanuel, God *with* us. God is not only good when he takes away the pain, but he is also good in the midst of it.

I managed to acknowledge the Lord's presence on the first anniversary of Brian's death: "I have moments when I think I simply can't go on, but I do, and I'm so thankful to the Lord for his strength."

HAUNTING QUESTIONS

"Guilt is perhaps the most painful companion to death."

~ Elisabeth Kubler-Ross

Many questions haunt widows. The bottom line stays the same. If I had done something differently, could I have changed the outcome?

Pablo's wife, Maria, didn't pay much attention to her own health. She enjoyed her desserts, cooked family dinners, and enjoyed time with her grandkids. She began feeling more tired than normal and attributed it to age. Pablo suggested she check in with her doctor, but she didn't get around to it. She suddenly experienced a massive heart attack. After she arrived at the hospital, a second heart attack occurred, and she continued to decline. After her death, Pablo asked me if he should've insisted she go to the doctor. Could he have arrived at the hospital sooner? What if they had gone to a different hospital? Could Maria's death have been avoided?

What did I do to deserve this? Is this my fault?
Is God punishing me?

I wrote the following response to one widow who asked me if God was punishing her:

> I can tell you this is most likely not your fault; there is nothing you did to deserve it. At times God punishes because we refuse to walk with him and we dishonor his name, but I assume you've lived a normal Christian life, in which case this is filtered through God's love even though it doesn't feel like it. Remember how Job lost all of his children and possessions in one day? In Job's case, Satan tried to knock him down spiritually. God allowed it. God even recommended Job as the object of Satan's attack because God knew Job would remain faithful. I sometimes try to imagine difficulties as a compliment from God because he believes in me more than I believe in him.

Also, remember, scripture promises that "In this world we *will* have tribulation. But *take heart*. I have *overcome* the world" (John 16:33, emphasis mine). Death came as a result of sin in general. We will all die, and scripture says God already knew how many days your husband would live even before he was conceived. For the future, the end to death is the final victory, and we get to spend eternity making up for lost time with our loved ones who die before us.

For now, though, death brings great pain. During my worst times I clung to this verse: "Because of the Lord's great love we are not consumed, for his compassions never fail. They are new every morning" (Lam. 3:22–23).

Every day I felt like I could not go on, but every morning I got up and did it all over again. Just the fact that you can get up and do anything at this stage in your grief is a huge blessing, and God gives grace for each moment.

What If . . . ?

The "What if . . . ?" question haunts people relentlessly. If I had just gotten him to the hospital sooner . . . If she had just gone to see the doctor . . . If someone had stayed with him . . . If, if, if . . . In the end, we can't go back. Our loved one stays put in the grave, and we remain powerless to change it. How do we make sense of this fact?

Jerry Sittser admits he couldn't stop the "What ifs." Why didn't they leave just five minutes later or linger longer at a stop sign?[12] Maybe they could've avoided the accident that killed his mom, wife, and daughter. Sittser found comfort in the stories of Job and Joseph in the Old Testament. "Job finally beheld God's unfathomable greatness,"[13] and Joseph saw that although his brothers intended harm, God meant good. Sittser states that he chooses "to believe that there is a bigger picture and that my loss is part of some wonderful story authored by God himself."[14]

Personally, I derive the greatest comfort from Jesus' story at the Garden of Gethsemane (Luke 22). Jesus, knowing he had to suffer torture and death, first pleaded with his Father to deliver Him. He also knew salvation and forgiveness for all humanity required his death. Recognizing God's plan as much bigger than himself, he submitted to the Father's will.

When Brian battled against death, I battled with God's plan. What if Brian's death brought new life and forgiveness to one person to whom it would not have come if Brian lived? Who was I to ask God to save Brian's life for me and my family if God's plan included something greater? Or if it meant one person couldn't enjoy God's Kingdom? Would I be that selfish?

I wanted Brian to live more than anything. I also knew God doesn't waste hardship. If Brian's death brought greater good, how could I selfishly cling to my own desires? Would I willingly trust God with my worst fear?

The questions we should ask instead: What does God want to accomplish through this loss? Am I willing to trust him with it even though it hurts immensely?

More Food for Thought

If you find it difficult to ask what God wants to accomplish through this and you question your willingness to trust him, consider asking some more questions:

- Is God really good?
- Is God's character trustworthy?
- Is God all powerful?
- Does God really know all things?
- How can a good God allow bad things?

To help think these questions through and to find more answers, see my chapters on "Trust" and "Hope." In "Trust," I also list a number of books that address these questions in more depth and with greater eloquence than I can. All four authors do an excellent job in addressing these basic theological questions.

FEAR

"No one ever told me that grief felt so like fear."

~ *C.S. Lewis, A Grief Observed*

In his 1933 inaugural address, Franklin D. Roosevelt stated, "We have nothing to fear but fear itself." I don't know. Maybe that's profound for some. But the fear we experience as widows is pretty real. At least it feels awfully real to me.

Fear of Being Alone

Looking back, I marvel at my own bravery as a single woman prior to marriage. My mother worried about me. She worried about my lack of fear and lack of experience.

Once widowed, I marveled at my own fear and lack of bravery. Suddenly fear entered my life—in a very big way. I feared facing life alone, even with three children in my home. My faith remained strong, but my human anchor no longer lived in my world. Brian fought illness for so long, but his presence in our lives gave us emotional security and a sense of physical safety as well. His death snatched away our security blanket, and we felt vulnerable.

Fear of Managing Finances

My survey revealed that women most fear managing their finances. They hope their money holds out. I imagine this fear pertains mostly to women who don't work outside the home or women who don't make much money on their own. Both men and women whose spouse earned the bulk of the household income would likely experience fear when the income disappears due to their spouse's death.

Even when a large life insurance policy exists, or if plenty of money flows, the lone survivor feels fear with regard to the finances. Questions abound. Will I invest properly? Where do I go to invest the money? Whom can I trust? Will the money last?

Part of the problem lies with our state of mind. We find ourselves caught up in a whirlwind of emotions. Shock and confusion attack our brains in the early months following the death of our spouse, and we can't think straight. We find it difficult to just get out of bed, much less figure out what to do with our finances. Some suggestions:

- If you can, find a trusted friend or family member to help.
- Ask other widows for advice.
- Ask someone you trust to suggest a financial advisor.
- Talk to more than one financial advisor. Most won't charge to talk to you about a basic plan regarding your finances. It's part of the sales process. Make sure to take notes because you won't remember what she said.
- Pick a well-known company with a good track record.

Fear of Failure

What if I can't do this alone? What if I can't hold out sexually? How will my kids make it without a dad or mom? All of these logical questions—and many more—scurry through our minds on a daily basis.

The bottom line? It's hard, and we don't like it. We didn't choose these circumstances.

The truth? We can make it through a whole lot more than we think we can.

Fear of Other Deaths

Many people become obsessively protective after losing a loved one. Having faced the devastation of death, the person experienced with grief worries about the possibility of losing someone else we love. The natural tendency to cling to and try to control everyone around us warrants careful consideration.

My oldest son, a gymnast at the time of Brian's death, loves extreme sports and risk-taking. I watched in horror one night as a video showed up on Facebook. My teenage son enjoyed the ride of his life in a grocery cart pulled by a rope attached to a pick-up truck. Immediately, I picked up the phone and called him. I left a panicked message, telling Chad to get out of that dangerous grocery cart. I did not enjoy the idea of burying him next to his father. To my chagrin, this incident had taken place weeks before the Facebook post! Turns out, I panicked for nothing—after the fact.

This event, clearly a typical teenage ploy, was a little extreme. We probably all agree it qualified for a little terror on my part. But we must carefully watch our tendency to freak out over more mild events. I found myself worrying if Chad didn't make it home by the time I expected him. While he usually communicated with me, I regularly required myself to say a prayer and give him to the Lord. I couldn't control the outcome of his activities anyway, but I dreaded the thought of another loss.

Trusting the Lord with everyday details comes easier with time. I recommend you take note of your fears, whether rational or irrational, and practice committing them to your heavenly Father. We must avoid placing our personal fears on our loved ones. We draw great anger and frustration when we become overly protective.

Elizabeth Elliott famously encouraged her readers that God didn't give us grace for our imagination. He gives us grace for each day. "When I get to tomorrow's troubles, God will be there with sufficient grace. The problem with my imagination is that it always leaves God out of the equation. It always imagines a future in which God has forgotten to show up."[15]

> So do not fear, for I am with you; do not be dismayed, for I am your God. I will strengthen you and help you; I will uphold you with my righteous right hand.
>
> _Isaiah 41:10_

> The _Lord_ is my _light_ and my _salvation_
> Whom shall I fear?
> The _Lord_ is the _stronghold_ of my life
> Of whom shall I be afraid?
> _Wait_ for the _Lord_
> Be _strong_ and _take heart_ and
> _Wait_ for the _Lord_.
>
> _Psalm 27:1, 14_
> _(emphasis mine, from my journal)_

> Have no fear of sudden disaster . . . for the Lord will be your confidence.
>
> _Proverbs 3:25–26_

REGRET

"Let's face it. We all regret something. Perfection didn't exist in our marriages. Regret is a part of the grief process. The problem with death: It is absolutely and utterly irreversible. There's no rewind button. There's no opportunity to say 'I'm sorry' for the times we argued over stupid stuff. There's no option for reshuffling priorities. There's no chance to say 'I love you' one more time."

~ K. Howard Joslin

At first, I thought I avoided regret. During Brian's illness I purposed not to regret the way I treated him. I didn't want to lament time not spent with him. I didn't want to feel remorse over harsh words spoken. In my favor was the fact that I had time to appreciate every day and make conscious choices regarding how I treated Brian and guilt I didn't want to carry.

As time passes, however, memories jump to mind, and I wonder if I hurt him by this or that. I wonder if I upset him when I expressed frustrations over things he couldn't fix. Overwhelmed daily by the responsibility of caring for him as well as handling everything child-related, I regularly vented in his presence. I cannot ask him now if that hurt him. I can't now apologize. I can't go back and change one thing.

Caregivers

In the survey I conducted, many who cared for their spouses during illness expressed shame that they didn't show enough patience, or they wished they had been kinder. No doubt we all could've done a better job. If you served as caregiver, you also know the exhaustion and stress that comes with the task. Everything hinged on you.

Let's think for a minute what that job entailed. You probably did most—or all—of the following:

- Made all of the doctor appointments.
- Took your sick spouse to the doctor.
- Kept track of medical records, medications, and symptoms.
- Asked all the right questions.
- Kept the house clean (or at least tried).
- Did the grocery shopping.
- Made sure your lawn got mowed.
- Transported children to and from their activities.
- Spent time with your children.
- Prepared meals and cleaned up after them.

Do you get the picture? My sweet friend, Barbara, reminded me that my ability to remain on my feet bore witness to a miracle in itself.

If you treated your spouse poorly at times or got tired and frustrated, you demonstrated normalcy. While every caregiver has failed numerous times, we must find the ability to forgive ourselves. I don't want to excuse bad behavior, but we must accept the fact that we took on a completely exhausting job, both emotionally and physically. We can forgive ourselves for human failures.

Sudden Death

If your spouse died suddenly, you didn't get the chance to make apologies or think through potential regrets. Possibly you and your wife argued right before she died, and now you feel terrible guilt. Maybe your relationship needed a doctor and now nothing can fix it. You may be paralyzed by guilt.

We often give more grace to others than we give ourselves. Accept your inability to handle everything perfectly. God loves us and forgives us just as we are.

Forgiveness

My husband, Howard, and I reconcile our guilt by reminding ourselves that what hurt or angered Brian and Ann while here on earth, they now understand. As believers in the presence of God, they now forgive. We sought forgiveness from our

Lord and asked God to tell Brian and Ann we're sorry, and we miss them. We can't change the past, but we can learn from past failures, accept God's forgiveness, and make changes for the future.

The apostle Paul wrote, "Brothers and sisters, I do not consider myself yet to have taken hold of it [becoming perfect]. But one thing I do: *Forgetting* what is behind and *straining* toward what is ahead, I *press on* toward the goal to win the prize for which God has called me heavenward in Christ Jesus" (Phil. 3:13–14, emphasis mine).

> If we confess our sins, he is faithful and just and will forgive us our sins and purify us from all unrighteousness.
>
> *1 John 1:9*

> *Yet* he was *merciful*; he *forgave* . . . he *remembered* that they were *but flesh*.
>
> *Psalm 78: 38, 39*
>
> *(emphasis mine)*

VULNERABILITY

"Loss reduces people to a state of almost total brokenness and vulnerability. I did not simply feel raw pain; I was raw pain."

~Jerry Sittser

"Stripped of any illusion of self-sufficiency, I was deeply aware that I needed God's help with everything from breathing to buying cars."

~Lois Mowday Rabey

"I feel very vulnerable and uncomfortable around most men because I don't know what they will do. I want to be myself, but I'm fearful of men getting the wrong idea when I'm *so* not ready to start dating! When you're married, you feel safe under your husband's umbrella, but when you're forced into being single, it is an extremely scary and vulnerable place to be."

From my Journal Jan. 18, 2010

Vulnerable with the Opposite Sex

I foolishly trusted Harold, fifteen years my senior. He helped with the yard, and in my mind he fit in the fatherly figure category. Before I knew it, he called regularly and bought gifts for the kids and me. I should've caught on at that point.

One day he poured on the syrup and quipped, "You know I'm sweet on ya, don't you?"

I wanted to vomit. I asked him to stop, and when he didn't, I finally quit answering his calls and avoided him altogether.

It seems marriage provides a certain sense of safety. When we're secure in our marriages, we feel secure in other situations, including relationships with the opposite sex. When our marriage status suddenly flips to *widowed*, our sense of safety gets ripped from us as well, and we feel vulnerable. In some sick way, I found myself suddenly "available," the last place I wanted to be.

Where do I fit in? How will others treat me? I wondered. I wanted to know men find me attractive, but I couldn't handle hearing it from anyone but my husband, who no longer existed in my world.

I have another friend named Stan. Women flocked to him like geese. They manipulated situations to get close to him and faked the need for rides. They threw themselves at him just because he carried the title "widower."

This kind of ridiculousness puts us on the defensive and makes it even more difficult to maneuver our way through the web of widowhood.

Vulnerable to Strangers

I found myself afraid to answer the door and didn't want to give any personal information to anyone, even for business reasons. I feared letting others know I was alone. Vulnerability made me fearful.

Emotionally Vulnerable

People regularly ask questions. I tend to relay my feelings honestly, but I found this unsafe. Though many people asked how we were doing, few seemed to really want the truth. Navigating the pain of loss with the realization that others rarely care enough to listen to what we truly feel drags us down even more. Why do people ask if they don't want to know?

I think it's a matter of courtesy. They know they should ask because we suffered a huge loss. They do care, but they can't enter into the pain with us. They politely ask and secretly hope we'll just say, "Fine." They did their duty by showing concern, but they didn't plan for an exit in case we pour out our bucket of pain on them, causing them to feel uncomfortable.

In our grief, we naturally assume our friends wouldn't ask how we are if they didn't really want the truth. We feel overjoyed to think someone cares, and so we dump the entire bucket of our souls on them. The conversation often ends abruptly and awkwardly for all. The "friend" walks away feeling embarrassed that he didn't know what to say, while we walk away feeling stabbed in the heart.

Vulnerable to the Phone

I don't know about you. Maybe you don't experience all of this craziness, but I constantly felt vulnerable. If I answered the phone, I risked hearing hurtful words on the other end. Or I risked the responsibility of something being asked of me.

I didn't feel capable of handling either one. As much as possible, I stayed off the phone or let it go to voice mail. Honestly, I lived in a prison of my own making, but it felt safer to me than the outside world.

As mentioned in other chapters, I chose to respond to phone calls mostly through e-mail.

Vulnerable to Loneliness

Because feelings overwhelmed me, I felt vulnerable to my own loneliness, which dragged me down emotionally. But I couldn't stop it. Grief totally saps our dignity, as we seem powerless to control it.

We feel so out of control that we wish we could end all the craziness. Unfortunately, we must persevere and submit to the time it takes to grieve. But take heart! This level of vulnerability decreases with time as we gain more confidence, and the weightiness of grief diminishes.

> There is a time for everything, and a season for every activity under heaven . . . A time to weep and a time to laugh, a time to mourn and a time to dance. . . . He has made everything beautiful in its time.
>
> *Ecclesiastes 3:1, 4, 11*

EMOTIONAL SUPPORT

"You have to learn where your pain is. You have to burrow down and find the wound, and if the burden of it is too terrible to shoulder, you have to shout it out; you have to shout for help . . . And then finally, the way through grief is grieving."

~Jane Hamilton

We widows typically feel all alone and often fall into deep depression. I highly recommend finding a way to help alleviate the loneliness. Talking to others who know how to help us or to those who experience the same kind of pain encourages tremendously.

Counseling

Counseling usually occurs one-on-one. If you already know a good counselor, it's easier to make an appointment to see him or her. When we don't know where to look for a good counselor, we often feel confused and overwhelmed.

I admit it took visiting with numerous counselors before we found one who fit our family. Over time, I kept looking, asking friends, and trying new ones. At first, I went with a counseling ministry in a large church. Next, I tried someone covered by insurance. Both scenarios ended up frustrating me. Eventually we found a great guy who, with God's help, saved our family.

In a counseling session we have the full attention of the counselor and can address our own needs without worrying about what other people feel or hear. I chose counseling because I needed anonymity. My family is well-known in the area, and I needed to deal with my pain in a private setting. But we spent a fortune in the process. If you can't afford private counseling, don't let this deter you.

Churches, especially large ones, generally provide counseling services. Sometimes these churches charge according to your income—on a sliding scale. Even though counseling through a local church didn't meet my needs long term, I recommend starting by contacting churches near you. If they don't provide counseling services, they can usually recommend someone.

Insurance plans ordinarily cover some form of counseling, including Christian counseling. The key? Find someone to fit your personality and individual needs.

If you need counseling, keep looking until you find a secure, comfortable situation. The search proves difficult sometimes, but the benefits outweigh the negatives, once you settle on someone.

Support Groups

A faith-based, nationally-known grief recovery group called GriefShare exists specifically for the grieving. The creators of this program developed it exclusively to help those who lose loved ones. When we walk into one of these groups, we immediately join those who know and understand our pain.

Most friends I know who've attended GriefShare highly recommend it. They find great relief from meeting with fellow grievers on a weekly basis. The program lasts thirteen weeks, but the schedule is organized so that you can join at any point in the thirteen-week program. GriefShare.org lists locations near you.

The hard part, I know, comes when we must force ourselves to attend something outside our comfort zone, or simply just outside our home. When we're bound up by our grief, we don't want to walk into any place alone for any reason. I understand this. The problem with giving in to these fears? We don't find help, and we continue to spiral downward.

If you can't face going to a group alone, find a friend or family member willing to attend with you. Crying at a GriefShare meeting—or in a counseling setting—is normal, so you can join the crowd in safety.

Widows Support Groups

Try searching online for "widows groups" or "widows support groups + your town (or one nearby)." Likely something will pop up. To my knowledge no nationally known program exists for widows, at least not on the same scale as the GriefShare ministry. I found some groups on the rise, but no nationally known, faith-based widows' organizations exist that I could find.

What does this mean? Most widow support groups exist as independent organizations. This may not mean anything bad necessarily, but we must use discernment when attending something not sponsored by a larger organization or church—unless we know the people involved.

That said, I started a widows' group myself. I began with three friends who needed a safe setting in which to share their pain. I met with these women anyway, so it made sense to group them together. We began by meeting at my house.

But please carefully handpick the widows who attend if you plan to host a group in your home. You must protect yourself, as some people will take advantage. I found a church willing to sponsor our group. This took the pressure off of announcing my home address to possible strangers.

Another consideration—do you want to participate in a mixed-gender group or not? Honestly, I doubt if many groups exist for men only. Women-only groups are much more prevalent simply because more female widows exist compared to their male counterparts.

I recommend faith-based groups because they should stand for high morals and good choices. Plus they embrace the true reason for hope.

Jesus' Example

I find enormous comfort in Jesus' expression of emotion:

> And he came out and went, as was his custom, to the Mount of
> Olives, and the disciples followed him. And when he came to the
> place, he said to them, "Pray that you may not enter into temptation."
> And he withdrew from them about a stone's throw, and knelt down
> and prayed, saying, "Father, if you are willing, remove this cup
> from me. Nevertheless, not my will, but yours, be done." And there
> appeared to him an angel from heaven, strengthening him. And being
> in agony he prayed more earnestly; and his sweat became like great
> drops of blood falling down to the ground. And when he rose from
> prayer, he came to the disciples and found them sleeping from sorrow,
> and he said to them, "Why are you sleeping? Rise and pray that you
> may not enter into temptation" (Luke 22:39–46 ESV).

Notice how Jesus first asks the disciples to pray that they won't fall into temptation. When Jesus then withdraws to pray by himself, he asks the Father to rescue him from death. Instead, his Father sends an angel to strengthen him.

I always assumed Jesus Christ didn't need strengthening. After all, he was God's son. God the Father sent an angel, who strengthened Jesus and then—*after receiving strength from the angel*—Jesus continued to plead with the Father even *more* earnestly. This time, instead of showing *strength*, he pleaded with the Father to the point that sweat drops of blood poured from his body to the ground. Jesus expressed greater emotion than any other human throughout history.

Jesus proved that we can trust God, yet still express intense emotion. Take heart when you read this. Jesus submitted to his Father's will, and knowing the pain ahead, he expressed deeper emotion than you or I will ever experience. Let me encourage you that the deep expression of emotion and grief fits within the realm of godliness. When friends tell you to "just trust God," remind them that Jesus pleaded with the Father to rescue him from death, even *after* receiving strength through an angel. Jesus submitted to the Father's will, but he didn't like it.

I believe we are free to express our emotion even to the point where we sweat drops of blood like Jesus did. We don't have to like where we find ourselves. Expressing emotion doesn't indicate a lack of faith. It simply signifies grief. We can love God and submit to his plan, but we don't have to like it.

Jesus proved that grief comes naturally, and it can coexist with faith. Jesus never questioned God's goodness, and he never sinned, yet he poured out his heart to his Father, pleading with him to change the plan. Instead, God gave him strength.

My application summary of Luke 22:

- **Pray** honestly as Jesus did.
- **Trust** God's character even when bad things happen.
- **Understand** that his plan is bigger than we are and bigger than our own feelings or pain.
- **Believe** that when God chooses not to deliver he does provide strength.
- **Understand** that God's strengthening process doesn't always take away the pain.
- **Submit** to God's plan no matter what that might mean.

Save me, O God for the waters have come up to my neck. I sink in the miry depths where there is no foothold. I have come into the deep waters; the floods engulf me. . . . But, I pray to you, O Lord. . . . Do not let me sink.

Psalm 69:1–2; 13–14;

You are my help and my deliverer; O Lord, do not delay.

Psalm 70:5

Know that the Lord is God. It is he who made us, and *we are his*; we are his people, the sheep of his pasture. *Enter* into his gates with thanksgiving, and his courts with praise; give thanks to him and praise his name. For the Lord is *good* and his Love *endures forever*; his *faithfulness continues* through *all* generations.

Psalm 100:3–5

(emphasis mine)

Section Four

HUMAN INTERACTIONS

RELATIONSHIPS

"Grief lasts longer than sympathy, which is one of the tragedies of the grieving."

~Elizabeth McCracken

"The one thing you can count on in life is change," says an old adage. Sadly, relationships regularly change as well, especially in the aftermath of death. Some friends can handle our emotional ups and downs, while others simply cannot. They seem to need us happy. It makes their lives easier.

Some folks listen intently with compassion. Others change the subject when we talk about our pain or break down in tears. Some ask how we're doing but, really, they just want to hear, "I'm fine." They don't know how to respond or don't want to engage with us. They find it too painful or awkward.

Talk about reasons for frustration! The time in our lives when we need our friends and family relationships the most, they often fall apart. People continually respond in self-centered, uninformed, or inexperienced ways.

Human Nature

Honestly, I raged with anger toward people who could not support me in my hour of greatest need. I couldn't understand why a supposedly concerned friend would ask how the kids and I managed, but before I could formulate an answer, she walked away. Others gave their time to come and "help" in my home but spent the time criticizing me.

We need supportive people in our lives, yet, unfortunately, people are fallible. It takes a lot of energy, kindness, and selflessness to walk through grief with a friend. Many just cannot enter our pain with us. They tend to avoid our pain altogether or try to fix our problems, something no magic wand can quickly or easily solve. Try to keep in mind that the problem lies with your friend, not you. Forgive them for their humanity. This does not mean, however, that you need to continue inviting them to hurt you.

Play It Safe

Many people will politely ask how you are doing. But the sad truth is, most don't really want the honest answer—or maybe they just don't know what to do with it. Or maybe they don't have the time to hear the answer.

Far too often I stood alone, baffled by the insensitivity of those who quickly disappeared after asking a very personal and emotionally charged question, which left me feeling confused, hurt, and exposed. I finally learned not to answer directly, and certainly not with details.

My advice? Gently reply, "Very well, considering." Those who need you okay, and those who can't empathize will readily accept your answer and likely walk away. Those willing to bear your burdens will ask more questions. You will quickly discover whom you can trust with the details.

Fix-It Friends

My friend Eve couldn't stand to see me sad. She continually encouraged me to date, justifying it by exclaiming, "But you're so hot!" This infuriated me on so many levels. She communicated to me: I owe some man my body; looks make all the difference; I can just pick a man and start dating; it doesn't matter how I feel. What ridiculous, illogical thinking!

Mind you, Eve had honorable intentions. She heard statistics indicating an unmarried woman's chances of remarriage go down after five years of singleness. Instead of quietly trusting God with her concerns about my situation, she tried to fix it without considering my feelings. She didn't understand my need to grieve, nor did she consider the fact that I couldn't randomly pick another man to fill the hole in my heart. I finally told her, "I'm going to be sad for a while. I need you to be okay with it."

Instead of listening and hearing our pain, too many people want to jump in and fix things for us. They think if they fix our problem, their concern disappears as well. They can't stand the uncomfortable feelings our pain causes them.

If your friend regularly offers solutions in an effort to fix everything, try to gently explain what you need from him or her. If your friend drains your energy and makes you feel bad, take a break for a while. Spend your time focusing on encouraging and helpful friends.

Critical Friends

"O Lord, I need to keep my eyes on you! People keep letting me down. I wish I knew better how to deal with all of the unwanted advice and criticism," I wrote in my journal. Job's friends did well, as long as they kept their mouths shut and just sat there with him. When they opened their mouths, they became hurtful and accusatory.

Interestingly, God required Job to ask forgiveness for his friends even though they hurt him deeply. God asked Job to pray on behalf of the friends for forgiveness, but Job doesn't tell us whether he continued a relationship with them.

Ponder this: "After Job prayed for his friends, the Lord made him prosperous again" (Job 42:10). Isn't that interesting? I don't think we can assume God will automatically prosper us if we ask forgiveness for our insensitive friends. Scripture tells us over and over again, however, to forgive so that our sins will be forgiven (Matt. 6:14; Mark 11:21–25; Luke 6:37; 2 Cor. 2:10–11).

Family

Family, especially the family of the deceased, grieves along with you. Unfortunately, everyone grieves differently and each person experiences different needs. Family relationships are notorious for becoming difficult in the aftermath of a death. Because widows regularly encounter difficult family relationships, I address the issues of "Kids" and "In-laws" in separate chapters.

Phone-Shy

I've mentioned this before. I all-but-completely shied away from the phone after Brian died. I heard entirely too many hurtful comments over the phone. Already an emotional wreck, I could no longer risk what might come out of someone else's mouth. I mostly let phone calls go to voice mail. Granted, I rarely checked voice mail, but I found it easier to hear the need or request before responding. This practice frustrated others at times, but I couldn't cope any other way.

Instead of returning phone calls, I usually responded with e-mails. I simply couldn't handle surprises over the phone. It took less emotional energy to send an e-mail.

In the midst of your difficult emotional state, feel free to handle communication in a manner that best suits your needs. Ask God for wisdom to help you respond in a godly manner. Always show kindness when setting boundaries. As long as you treat others with respect, they hold no justification for objecting to your behavior.

Helpful Suggestions

- Rely on those who will listen, encourage, and support you. Try not to drive any one person nuts, however. You need support, but no one can meet your every need. Four or five people in my life willingly listened as I poured out my sorrow. I rotated calling them so they wouldn't get tired of me. Thankfully, they graciously listened and continually showed me love.

- When you expose something personal and deep, you need a listener, not an instructor. If your friends try to instruct, gently tell them you need a listener. Exasperated at times, I wanted to scream, "I lost my husband, not my brains!"

- A social person by nature, I became much quieter and more withdrawn because grief took so much out of me. This is normal and okay for a time. But cautiously force yourself to enter social arenas little by little.

- Tell your friends you love hearing their stories about your spouse. Many fear upsetting you and avoid the subject, as if you aren't already upset and thinking about your loss constantly. Even now, it means the world to me to hear someone say they miss something about Brian or that they think about him. Sometimes I still cry because it touches my heart that, not only do they remember, but they also took the time to share it. Every time my missionary friend comes home from Mexico, he talks about Brian's laugh. We all laugh while he tries to imitate it. I will be sad when that stops.

- It may sound harsh, but at some point we must figure out this new life between us and God. That does not mean you won't talk to your loving friends and family, but you will become less dependent on them as time passes.

Relating to Others

When you wonder how to relate to others, keep in mind that, "Each of you should look not only to your own interests, but also to the interests of others" (Phil. 2:4).

Even if someone deeply hurts you, carefully and lovingly express your need without returning the hurt.

Your friends need you, too. Try to listen to your friends even though you may find it difficult to focus on them. As much as possible, let them know you care about their needs as well. They still need your friendship, even if they willingly put their own needs aside for a while.

We can't possibly be all things to all people in the midst of our sorrow. God has us in this place for this time. We don't need to feel guilty about our needs.

If it is possible, as far as it depends on you, live at peace with everyone.

Romans 12:18

IN-LAWS

"But grief makes a monster out of us sometimes . . . And sometimes you say and do things to the people you love that you can't forgive yourself for."

~ Melina Marchetta

Lois works with military widows and says they complain most about conflict with their in-laws. Helena relayed how her mother-in-law moved in with her after her husband's death to take his place in the parenting role. When Helena chose five years later to remarry, her mother-in-law refused to move out.

Emma's in-laws feel the need to help others in their pain. They showed up at her door—often unannounced—to "help," at times when she and her children needed solitude and time to figure out how to function without the head of their household. It offended and hurt her that they wanted to come on their time schedule, and on their terms, without considering her needs and schedule. When she did ask for help, they criticized and accused. Finally, she couldn't take it anymore. Frustrated, hurt, and angry she asked them to back off.

Expectations

Numerous reasons exist for conflict with in-laws. In my opinion, the main problem occurs because each party adheres to a different set of expectations. We may perceive their role in our lives and/or that of our children one way, while they perceive it in a completely different way. They may expect us to need their help, while we want to manage on our own. Or, we need their help but their grief renders them incapable of reaching out to us.

Grief

Joleen's in-laws don't easily express emotions. They often changed the subject when she mentioned her husband's name. Their needs were opposite from hers.

Joleen couldn't handle talking about other things, as if her husband never existed. In her mind it honored her husband, Josiah, to talk about him. She felt lost without him. Her entire world had been turned upside down, and she didn't know how to exist apart from Josiah. Joleen couldn't understand the need her in-laws craved to change the subject. But she couldn't change them or their needs, which were as real as hers.

Our spouse's parents will likely grieve differently than we do. The differences in needs and desires can offend one or both parties. Everyone deserves the right to grieve their own way, and we should respect one another's needs. But complications naturally arise when needs vary.

Rights

In-laws may feel the right or responsibility to help rear children who still live at home. As in Helena's case, the in-laws may feel they've lost their voice in your home with the loss of their child who represented their values. What they may neglect to realize—or honor—is that you represent the values on which you and your spouse agreed.

Our in-laws need to respect and trust us with the choices we make since their child chose us as their partner. Although it can be a difficult dance, all involved need to understand one another's unique role, rights, and needs.

Control

The issue of control runs a close second to that of expectations when it comes to causing conflict. Control issues connect with feelings of entitlement and/or the inability to let adult children make their own choices. Sadly, mother-in-law jokes exist for a reason.

Some mothers-in-law get a bad reputation for causing trouble because they can't give up control of their adult children. If this problem occurred before their adult child died, it will most certainly continue after the adult child's death. They couldn't control the circumstances surrounding the death of their child, so they often grasp for control wherever they can.

Good Intentions

Try to keep in mind that, even though your in-laws may not always comply with how you want or need to be treated, they usually have the right intentions. They want to help. The problem? Communication. Many don't know how to navigate discussing their desires and needs with you appropriately, and unfortunately, it can backfire. Remember they are human just like you. The fact that they may not know how to treat you properly doesn't necessarily dub them "bad people."

Boundaries

If at all possible, sit down and talk about expectations, desires, and needs. Try to come up with acceptable solutions. If you can't come to mutually agreeable terms, set your own boundaries and insist on them for your own sanity.

Remember that they grieve, too. Even if they hurt your feelings, you must respond to them in the kindest possible manner. Use the following scriptures as a guide:

- "Keep your tongue from evil and your lips from speaking lies" (Psalm 34:13).
- "Sin is not ended by multiplying words, but the prudent hold their tongues" (Prov. 10:19).
- "A fool finds pleasure in evil conduct, but a person of understanding delights in wisdom" (Prov. 10:23).
- "Do not repay anyone evil for evil. Be careful to do what is right in the eyes of everybody. If it is possible, *so far as it depends on you*, live at peace with everyone. Do not take revenge, my friends, but leave room for God's wrath, for it is written: 'It is mine to avenge; I will repay,' says the Lord" (Rom. 12:17–19, emphasis mine).

I recommend a number of helpful books that talk about setting boundaries and dealing with difficult relationships:

- *The Emotionally Destructive Relationship: Seeing It, Stopping It, Surviving It* by Leslie Vernick
- *Bold Love* by Dr. Dan Allender & Dr. Tremper Longman, III
- *Boundaries: When to Say Yes, When to Say No, to Take Control of Your Life* by Henry Cloud and John Townsend

Grandparents

Unless danger exists, you must always allow your children access to their grandparents. Grandparents have a right to a relationship with their grandchildren. And your children need a relationship with their grandparents, if for no other reason than to honor their deceased parent.

If the children are young, schedule times to take them to see their grandparents for a visit or allow the grandparents to pick up the kids. You don't need to participate in the activity, especially if you find it difficult relating to them. You may set boundaries and communicate with them via e-mail or text, but make sure your anger and hurt don't transfer to the children.

Grandparents can communicate directly with older children and set times to get together outside of your presence. They can pick up the children or meet somewhere else with teenagers who drive.

CHILDREN AND DEATH

"We all died that day,
But only he went on.
The rest of us were left to haunt the earth,
Our moans and sobs sending people in every direction.
Food came to us in masses, But the dead don't eat.
We kept it just in case one of us resurrected.
Every last lasagna went into the trash.
We continued to possess our bodies,
And no one noticed we weren't us."

~Nikki Geiger

This poem, written by my daughter at the age of seventeen, reflects on her dad's death when she was only ten. She remembers well the pain of loss because she continues to feel its effects. This chapter could take up an entire book, but I will try to keep it to the basics.

Small Children

Small children may react differently on the outside from older—or even grown—children, although they feel the impact just as greatly. Small children tend to act out their feelings with bad behavior because they aren't as adept at expressing feelings with words.

I will say it one more time: When children lose one parent to death, they lose the other to grief. As the surviving parent, we must do everything in our power to show up on a daily basis for our kids. In our grief and brokenness, we tend to withdraw or yell. I did both.

I couldn't handle the daily rigors of parenthood alone. I found it easier to let the kids spend too much time on screens than to engage with them. I knew better, so I set time limits, but when they tested the limits, I lost my temper. They lied about their time limits. I couldn't prove it, so they often got away with it. I couldn't muster the strength to monitor their every move, and they figured it out.

Children need honesty. I tried from the very beginning of Brian's illness to share honestly with my kids, without giving too much information. Early on when asked if he would die, I told them he might die from this cancer, but the doctors told us it wouldn't be soon. As the time drew near, I tried to prepare them, but they didn't really hear me—probably because they didn't want to.

Only my youngest had not yet reached her teen years when her dad died. At just ten, however, she experienced early puberty, which brought with it a new set of trials. She suffered huge mood swings and bouts of anger that scared us all.

I clung to the Lord for wisdom in dealing with my own sorrow, as well as that of my children. My journal cries out to the Lord for help on a regular basis. The best advice I can give? Cling to the Lord daily. Ask for help from loved ones and friends. Read books, love your kids, listen to them, hold them accountable without being too harsh, and get them—and yourself—counseling if you can afford it. Hang on tight. Eventually, you *will* get through it.

Teenagers

Thankfully, my kids—ages seventeen, fourteen, and ten when their dad died—didn't turn to drugs, alcohol, or sex. One turned to sports and the other two to computers and video games. As mentioned above, even though they spent too much time playing video games, at least we accomplished our main goal—to make it until the next day. In the beginning we simply needed to survive.

My kids banded together those first months because hanging out with friends proved frustrating. Their friends didn't know what to say, and conversations or visits usually ended awkwardly. When their friends tried to show compassion and empathy, they insulted my kids by comparing the death of an animal or grandparent to the death of their parent. My kids knew better. They'd already lost animals and a grandparent, but they were ill-equipped to address these issues with their friends. Some of their friendships faltered.

Teens, in general, want to appear normal. They don't want to stand out in the crowd. In order to fit the norm, my kids often remained silent. Thus, "We continued to possess our bodies, and no one noticed we weren't us." They went through the motions of pretending, but they felt like walking carcasses, possessing bodies while trying to maintain equilibrium. The pain came out at home.

Homework became all but impossible to accomplish. Sleep eluded everyone each night. They got up and went to school, but exhaustion stole their ability to cope.

I marvel that anyone made it through that first school year. My oldest, the gymnast, hid his pain and functioned fairly normally, I think, because he worked out every day. Sports absorbed much of his angst, although he dealt with numerous injuries including a concussion, and he contracted meningitis. He graduated from high school less than a year after his dad's death and feared leaving me alone to manage the others. He chose community college.

My second child entered high school just three weeks after Brian died. His first-period teacher felt so sorry for him, he let him sleep through most classes. This child, unhealthy from infancy, just couldn't cope. Already grappling with ADHD and asthma, and although his IQ soars, he struggled just to pass the ninth grade. I spent months—years, actually—taking him to doctors, counselors, and psychiatrists trying to find the right solution for his troubles. Finally, after his eighteenth birthday, we discovered a thyroid condition, and his life improved greatly when he started taking medication for it.

After Brian's death I tried to talk openly with the kids and let them know they could talk about their dad and their pain with me. I think they tried to protect me because I always cried. Every now and then, they would talk to me about it. Though I tried my best to listen, I couldn't always contain the tears. It broke my heart because I felt the same things they felt—loneliness, fear, the inability to focus or sleep, and on the list goes.

I prayed with them when they shared their pain, and we limped along, one day at a time.

Grown Children

Grown children can cause their own trouble when we lose our spouse. Some become bossy and treat us like children. Some get greedy, and think they own rights to our stuff and our time. Some want us to quit moping around; they push us to move on. Others may join us in our grief.

Graciously express your needs to your grown children. Explain that you need them to understand your needs. Set boundaries if necessary, or ask them to visit now and then. Many older widows shared with me their disappointment in the fact that their grown children are too busy for them.

Tell your children you need them, but also try to understand their time is often limited. Maybe you can go to lunch or dinner with a different child each week. Try to work out a scenario that works for both parties so you don't feel abandoned and they don't feel overwhelmed.

If you have grandchildren, offer to babysit now and then. Children, in small doses, can bring great joy! I thought I could talk my mom into coming to live with me after Brian died. Both of us widows, I thought it would salve the loneliness for both of us.

One of my sisters has grandkids. Mom couldn't leave her great grandkids and move to Texas. The great grandkids gave her a reason to keep going.

Single Parenting

A year and a half after Brian's death, my journal read, "Mad, mad, mad!!!! I feel *really* angry tonight! It seems I am sad, crying, or angry! I thought I was doing better, and maybe I'm accomplishing tasks better, but this single parenting thing is about to do me in!!! I haven't been angry at Brian before, but tonight after Nikki's counseling session, I feel extremely angry with Brian. It is totally unfair that I have to deal with all of this on my own!"

The reality hit me hard. My oldest son, Chad, crashed a four-wheeler and couldn't remember the experience. The concussion took away his memory of the fact that he had lost his dad, and he grieved as if for the first time. The doctor recommended I take him to the emergency room.

Just as we headed out the door for the ER, Nikki began complaining of a headache and chills. Oh, great! I had one child who needed emergency medical care and another one running a fever, who needed tender loving care at home! I couldn't meet both needs, and the irony of it all socked me in the gut at that moment. I am, indeed, a single parent. This is the drill.

Single parenting can definitely test every fiber in us. I remember telling friends, "These kids are driving me to my knees!" Actually, that's exactly where God wants us and where we should go. On our knees before our heavenly Father, asking for his guidance, help, and strength.

The trauma of loss, coupled with the task of single-parenting, ranks extremely high on the stress monitor. Clinging to the Lord, hanging on to his promises, and coercing one foot in front of the other forces us to cope.

What Kids Need

Keep in mind that your children grieve, too. They simply show it differently than adults do, and over time grief presents in many different ways. Children grieve in smaller portions than we do, and they tend to process their grief about a year behind us.[16] They continue to grieve, just as we do. They don't "get over it." Don't let them fool you.

The bottom line? Our children need us. We must show up for them even if it means faking it. They need a healthy mix of discipline, grace, and love.

As I say in my blog entry, "Death: From the Mouth of Just a Babe":

Please do not let the smiles on Sunday morning at church or the laughter you see at school fool you. It's all a sham. These kids will experience loss for the rest of their lives.

Every birthday.

Every Mother's Day.

Every graduation.

Every wedding.

Every new baby.

The one person they wish could attend will silently decline the invitation.

But Jesus called the children to him and said, "Let the little children come to me, and do not hinder them, for the kingdom of God belongs to such as these."

Luke 18:16

Start children off on the way they should go, and even when they are old they will not turn from it.

Proverbs 22:6

Fathers [or mothers], do not exasperate your children; instead, bring them up in the training and instruction of the Lord.

Ephesians 6:4

GRIEF AND THE WORKPLACE

"Grief is always death's travelling companion."

~Robert C. DeVries

"Life is not set up for death," I told Shannon, whose husband died of cancer during the summer break—just weeks before she had to "put on her happy face" and return to teaching for the fall semester. It seems the American culture—and our employee benefit packages—don't consider the aftereffects of death.

Work Expectations

Women typically get six weeks off from work when they give birth to a baby—a joyful experience. Even new dads can take at least a six-week paternity leave. But if their spouse dies, an employee gets a maximum of three days off to deal with the worst experience of his life. Something is deeply wrong with this system.

If our spouse dies after a long illness, we must return to work while still reeling from the events of the weeks and months preceding our love's death. Whether his death occurred suddenly or after a long illness, we go back to work in a state of shock, feeling like our world came crashing down around us. Yet the expectation remains that we perform up to par in our jobs.

"You can't park your grief at the office door and then pick it up at five," explains Russel Friedman, author of the *Grief Recovery Handbook*. "When your heart is broken your head doesn't work right."[17]

Grief Support

Sadly, friends, family, and coworkers seem to assign time limits to grief. One year should suffice, and then we should "move on." One year after her husband died, Shannon found herself reeling from the realization that she needed to find her identity as a single person. This in itself brings grief. Shannon's superior told her she should readily take on extra tasks by now because, "after all, it's been a whole year."

My friend Kinsey lost her son in an accident. Her husband's company hired an assistant for him. The management told him to feel free to leave work if the pain became too much to bare. For two or three years he regularly left early, and the assistant stepped in to manage the tasks. What a wonderfully understanding—and accommodating—organization. If we all received that kind of support, we could at least feel the freedom to grieve as needed.

A Note to Coworkers and Loved Ones

Grief takes a very long time. If you read this book because you love someone who lost a spouse, hear this please. The second year is almost always harder than the first. The first year socks us with confusion, lack of focus, tears, survival mode, taking care of the business side of things, and a fog that holds us blanketed in a semi-co-matose state of mind.

Usually in the second year the fog lifts, reality hits, and depression kicks in. In year two we find ourselves working through how to keep going alone, the reality that we're single although we feel married, career considerations, whether or not to stay in our home, how to manage single parenting, and how to survive debilitating depression at the same time others need us to "move on."

Needs of the Grieving

What we really need: Patience, compassion, encouragement that we can do this, lots of prayer, and understanding from our friends. We need a listening ear, encouraging words, people who can give us the freedom to grieve, and those who willingly walk beside us through the process, but who don't offer advice where they have no experience.

If companies allow new parents to take off at least six weeks for the delivery of a baby and others readily understand that it takes six weeks to recover from any kind of surgery, why not allow widows at least six weeks for the amputation of our partner from our life? An amputation of a limb takes months of therapy and hard work before a person can function very well again. It is no different when death severs our marriages.

Again, Friedman laments, "Three days is a tragedy. Some companies are extraordinary and have big hearts when it comes to giving time off after a death, but many are stuck in the dark ages."[18]

What to Do

As I've said before, gently explain the challenges of grief to your friends, family, and coworkers. Tell your boss you will do your absolute best, but you need her to understand how grief affects you.

Share your own personal needs with those around you. Ask them to read this book to help them understand your life and needs. Talk to them about what they learned and what they might not understand. Let them know how your needs are similar or different from the stories in the book.

Train others to understand loss. It might just make a difference in your world.

I remain confident of this:
I will see the goodness of the Lord in the land of the living. Wait for
the Lord; be strong and take heart and wait for the Lord.

Psalm 27:13, 14

The Lord is close to the brokenhearted and saves those who are crushed in spirit.

Psalm 34:18

I lift up my eyes to the mountains—where does my help come from? My help comes from the Lord, the Maker of heaven and earth. He will not let your foot slip—he who watches over you will not slumber; indeed, he who watches over Israel will neither slumber nor sleep. The Lord watches over you—the Lord is your shade at your right hand; the sun will not harm you by day, nor the moon by night. The Lord will keep you from all harm—he will watch over your life; the Lord will watch over your coming and going both now and forevermore.

Psalm 121

Section Five

CHOICES TO CONSIDER

WEDDING RINGS

"Youth offers the promise of happiness, but life offers the realities of grief."

~ Nicholas Sparks, The Rescue

I t amazes me how the seemingly simple task of removing jewelry can leave a person feeling insecure, fearful, vulnerable, and exposed.

"Do you think it's time for me to remove my wedding rings?" Grace asked me four years after her husband's death. I sat speechless. How could I possibly tell her when she should make that decision?

Decisions

I can think of very few acts more gut-wrenching than choosing to physically remove the rings that signified our union. Some widows remove their wedding rings almost immediately, while others wear them until they themselves die. The decision, again, is completely *ours* to make. No one can even pretend to understand how we feel about our marriage, our love, our loss, or our grief.

Older women often choose to remain unmarried and wear their wedding rings until they die. Even though they may choose to remain single, most men in my survey removed their ring, stating simply, "I'm no longer married."

Shania loves her unique wedding set. She doesn't really want to wear her rings all the time, but she wears them on her right hand about once a month—around the date of her husband's passing. Her friends tell her she should wear them on his birthday instead of the date of his death. What do they know? She sometimes wears them for comfort, sometimes because of their beauty, and sometimes just to feel their weight on her finger. I say, do whatever makes *you* feel better.

Safety

I could not conceive of the idea of remarriage, and yet I felt as if I lied to the world by wearing my wedding rings. Although no longer married, I felt married and certainly didn't want the stigma of divorce. I felt vulnerable and didn't want men hitting on me in my despair, so I chose to wear my rings indefinitely. I could hide behind them for a while, at least. It felt safer.

Necessity

After much prayer and great sorrow, the excruciating decision to remove my wedding rings came when I caught myself spiraling downward emotionally. I desperately needed a way out of the downward spiral. My solution? To face it head on.

The first step to recovery—and therefore survival—seemed to require removal of the wedding rings from my finger and Brian's clothes from the closet. Maybe then I could *begin* to accept the reality of my singleness. And, in case it matters to you, that decision came nineteen months after Brian's death. According to my journal, I considered removing my rings an entire year before actually accomplishing it.

Respect

Out of respect to Brian's family I sent an e-mail to each one, informing them of this "excruciating decision." Although I retained every right to make the decision on my own, I didn't want them blindsided or thinking that this, in any way, meant I was over their son. I told them I would always love Brian, but I needed to find a way to move forward. They thanked me for the heads up and encouraged me in my decision.

If, for some reason, your in-laws, children, or friends give you flak about removing your wedding rings, simply tell them you intend no harm. You understand they hurt, too. You still love your deceased spouse, but this represents survival for you.

Replacement

Stella removed her wedding rings within a couple of months of her husband's death, but she replaced them with a generic sort of ring on another finger. Some will wear another ring in place of the wedding ring at first, and some move them to the right hand. Options definitely exist to help wean ourselves from our wedding rings in order to protect ourselves from vulnerability, as well as to soften the emotional blow.

Dating

Obviously, if you feel you would like to date and are emotionally ready to do so, it would probably make sense to remove your wedding rings. Grace said, "If someone gets to know me, he will know I'm not married." She was right, of course, but most men will not feel comfortable asking a woman for a date if she still wears her wedding rings. Most women wouldn't want to go out with a man who still wears his wedding rings either. Continuing to wear your rings on your left ring finger subtly indicates to a date that you really may not be ready to date.

DON'T BE STUPID

"We have a decision to make: keep trying to control a storm that is not going to go away or start learning to live within the rain."

~ Glenn Pemberton, Hurting with God

With grief comes the temptation to make stupid choices. In our deepest pain, we feel desperate to make it stop. Please respect yourself enough to behave wisely. I hear alarming stories where people behave badly in the midst of grief.

Force yourself to think—or at least act—rationally. "The best defense is offense," as they say, so make good choices before you get yourself into trouble. Carefully watch for these behaviors in your teenagers as well.

Abuse of Medication

On more than one occasion, the thought occurred to me: "I could take that entire bottle of pills and not worry about waking up tomorrow." My second thought, however, rebutted the first, "Your kids need you. You *must* get up." I never seriously considered actually following through on the temptation, but I certainly admit to thinking it.

As stated in the section titled "Prayer and Medication," we might benefit from proper use of medication for a while, but abuse only causes trouble. If you have a history of drug abuse, family history of drug abuse, or even fear the temptation to abuse medications talk to your doctor and let her help you construct a plan. Normal thoughts may include thoughts of taking a whole bottle of something. But normal behavior does not follow through on such thoughts.

Drug/Alcohol Abuse

Possibly the most common form of self-medication, at least in the United States, alcohol sits readily available on shelves everywhere we go, even at the pharmacy. I won't make the assumption that you think rationally at this point in your life.

Think about this: taking an antidepressant under your doctor's supervision is far better and safer than getting yourself stuck on something dangerous and addictive. Also, alcohol is a depressant. Do you want to risk feeling more depressed than you already are?

Scripture states clearly that we should "not get drunk on wine, which leads to debauchery. Instead, be filled with the Spirit" (Ephesians 5:18). The biblical mandate is to not get drunk. According to scripture we should focus our attention on filling ourselves with the Holy Spirit instead of allowing ourselves to fall into any form of depravity. When tempted to drown your sorrows, try drowning them in scripture.

Scripture will not take away your pain, but neither will drugs or alcohol. Addictions only compound our problems. Trying to focus on just one encouraging Bible verse, though, may give you a ray of hope.

Sex

Thousands of terribly sad stories arise from those who act out their pain by getting caught up in sexual relationships outside of marriage. It's normal and healthy to desire sex. Emotional and physical protection, however, require abstinence. Even if you don't believe in biblical abstinence outside of marriage, pure logic demands it.

I speak to this issue in much more detail in my chapter on "Sex" but, the Bible clearly mandates, "It is God's will that you should be sanctified; that you should avoid sexual immorality; that each of you should learn to control his own body in a way that is holy and honorable, not in passionate lust like the heathen, who do not know God...for God did not call us to be impure, but to live a holy life...he who rejects this instruction...rejects God" (1 Thess. 4:3–8).

The widow who lives for pleasure is dead even while she lives.

1 Timothy 5:6

Dating/Remarriage

Yes, the loneliness is unbearable, and the pain excruciating. Jumping into a new relationship too soon, however, usually ends in disaster. Glenn and Sofia married within the year after his wife died. Married now for more than 30 years, they admit to marrying a little too quickly. Author and counselor, Gary Smalley says, "Any new romantic relationship that comes within two years of the death of a spouse or divorce will most likely lead to additional pain, conflict, and heart damage."[19]

Do yourself a favor, and take time to grieve before allowing a new romantic relationship. Giving yourself time better equips you to make a good choice and experience the joys of love again. Too many make the assumption that getting married again will take away the grief or allow them to skip the grief process. Unfortunately, remarrying too quickly adds to the grief instead.

Pornography

Pornography traps and, as another addictive option, steals joy. Dr. Victor Cline indicates that sex and pornography can be a more difficult addiction to break than cocaine."[20] Wow! Do you really want to take that risk?

Instead, focus on God's character, his love and compassion for you, even in this pit. Pour out your heart to him. Hang on tight and allow him to renew your strength one tiny step at a time.

According to yourbrainonporn.com, "Not surprisingly, the most common tools employed [for recovery from porn addictions] include exercise, time in nature, creative activities, meditation, healthy diet, and socializing. Some of these naturally rewarding activities you can do by yourself, while others require human interaction."[21]

Financial

Shopping makes some of us feel better—until we realize how much we spent. Shopping can also develop into an addiction.

Cheryl's husband received half of the money from his life insurance policy at the time of his terminal diagnosis. Some insurance companies allow lump-sum distributions, depending on the policy, to help cover medical costs. Cheryl bought a house, put in a new kitchen, new floors, bought new furniture, new clothes, and just kept going. Although originally expected to die within two years, her husband, Jordan stabilized.

Suddenly, Cheryl realized most of the money had vanished, and she could no longer count on paying her bills. She ended up in a financial bind and had to sell their house before he even died.

Whether you receive life insurance money before or after your spouse's death, do not spend it without a budget. Don't squander what your spouse left to provide for you.

You may feel guilty that you "benefited" from your spouse's death. Remember he left this to provide for you out of love so you will not suffer financially. No matter the reason for your temptation to spend it all, resist the temptation and find a good financial counselor.

Tell only your financial counselor how much you receive from life insurance, especially if it's a lot of money. Too many people will actually establish a relationship with you just to get to your money.

I highly recommend a prenuptial agreement if you decide to remarry, especially if you inherited lots of money. You cannot afford to risk losing your nest egg to someone who might take advantage of you. A "pre-nup" also protects the money for your children, should you predecease your new husband. I hear too many stories where the kids received nothing when their last parent died because the step-parent took it all.

Believe me, I understand the temptation to make stupid choices. I understand the horrible waves of grief. I've been there.

Know this: it does not *feel* like God is a good God right now, but he is our only hope. Cling to him and cry out to him in your despair. Determine right now to hang on and not allow yourself to create more trouble for yourself by making stupid choices.

You can, and you will, get through this, but it takes time. Believe it or not, the more you try to mask your pain, the worse it turns out in the long run.

He gives strength to the weary and increases the power of the weak...
but those who hope in the Lord will renew their strength. They will soar
on wings like eagles; they will run and not grow weary; they will walk
and not be faint.

Isaiah 40:29, 31

SEX

Your bed seems terribly empty now. "Once it was a place of pleasure. Now there is just you, alone—without him—alone with your memories."

~ Jan Sheble

The death of a spouse brings with it many kinds of loss. The loss of our sexual relationship is "just another loss," said Jamal. Very few grief books dare address this issue. I conducted an anonymous survey and still found few widows and widowers willing to answer questions on sex. You know what this tells me? Widows feel guilty. They can't even answer the question anonymously, because they don't know what to do with their own sexual loss.

I hear grief affects the libido as well. For some, the intense grief masks their sexual drive for a time, while others find their sexual desires magnified. Both men and women wrestle with this issue. Let's look at what scripture says on the subject, and then we'll consider what it means for us widows.

One Flesh

From the very beginning of time, God made marriage a union that includes a sexual component. "For this reason a man will leave his father and mother and be united to his wife, and they will become one flesh" (Gen. 2:24). On three different occasions (to Adam and Eve, to Noah, and to Abraham) God told man to "be fruitful and increase in number," a task that's next-to-impossible without having sex. God created sex, and he fully expected husbands and wives to enjoy sexual activity.

Adultery

Adultery is "voluntary sexual intercourse between a married man and someone other than his wife or between a married woman and someone other than her husband."[22] Please don't kid yourself. Any kind of sexual activity between couples outside of marriage fits the sin category. Scripture makes it obvious. Do not commit adultery, even in your heart.

Too often, widows—out of loneliness—fall prey to relationships with married people. It usually happens because a kindhearted married person listens and cares about the widow's pain. Don't trust your broken heart to a married person of the opposite sex for any reason—except maybe in a counseling setting. Even then, be careful. Nothing good can come from a relationship with a married person.

- You have heard that it was said, 'You shall not commit adultery. But I tell you that anyone who looks at a woman lustfully has already committed adultery with her in his heart (Matt. 5:27–28).

- You know the commandments: 'You shall not murder, you shall not commit adultery, you shall not steal, you shall not give false testimony, you shall not defraud, honor your father and mother (Mark 10:19).

Fornication

Fornication is "consensual sexual intercourse between two persons not married to each other."[23] Scripture often references fornication by using the term "sexual immorality." The punishment for such behavior? Death. The Bible emphatically declares that we should abstain from fornication, or any kind of sexual activity outside of marriage.

- For out of the heart come evil thoughts—murder, adultery, sexual immorality, theft, false testimony, slander (Matt. 15:19).

- You are to abstain from food sacrificed to idols, from blood, from the meat of strangled animals and from sexual immorality (Acts 15:29).

- Dear friends, I urge you, as foreigners and exiles, to abstain from sinful desires, which wage war against your soul (1 Peter 2:11).

Trust

Other than biblical reasons for abstinence outside of marriage, I believe sex before marriage reigns as the biggest trust-buster in a relationship. How can we trust someone who willingly engages in sexual activity outside of marriage?

I tell my kids that a person who willingly waits for marriage to have sex with them is likely more trustworthy than one who won't wait. It shows depth of character, self-control, and respect for the partner. A relationship built on depth, instead of sex, stands the strongest. When sex enters the picture prior to marriage—or outside of marriage—trust is broken and becomes very difficult to regain.

Statistics back up this assertion. According to a Brigham Young University study, "Regardless of religiosity, waiting helps the relationship form better communication processes, and these help improve long-term stability and relationship satisfaction,"[24] or trust.

God gave us the gift of sex. He wants us to enjoy it, but within the bounds of marriage, where it bonds us together and provides a sense of trust and oneness. Outside of marriage, it does just the opposite.

Safety

I googled statistics on STDs, and found an unending amount of information. More widespread than the experts can calculate, staggering statistics persist. What shocks me? No one seems to consider this fact: if my partner willingly engages in sex with me outside of marriage, he likely engages in—or has engaged in—sex with numerous others. Why would anyone take such a high risk?

This kind of behavior is self-destructive and adds to your emotional pain, including guilt, another heartbreak, and possibly a destructive relationship. Respect yourself, including your emotional and physical health.

God set these standards for our protection, not out of meanness. When we hold to God's standards, safety is more achievable.

Forgiveness

According to the State of Dating report from 2014 conducted by ChristianMingle. com, 63 percent of Christian couples participate in sexual activity before marriage.[25] More and more Christian couples now live together prior to marriage, and if engaged, they justify that they are married in God's eyes.

My goal here is not to judge anyone, but to provide wisdom and hope. If sixty-three percent of couples have sex before marriage, then only thirty-seven percent choose to wait. If you participated in sex outside the bond of marriage, but you now recognize God's standard as just, right, and with your protection and best interest in mind, take heart. "If we confess our sins, he is faithful and just and will forgive us our sins and purify us from all unrighteousness" (1 John 1:9). No sin is too big for God's forgiveness.

Holy Sexuality

Christopher Yuan, author, recovered sex addict, and adjunct professor at Moody Bible College, points out that all humans struggle with lust, and no matter what our sexual desires, God calls us to "Holy Sexuality."[26] He says, "Be holy, for I am holy" (Lev. 11:44–45; 1 Peter 1:16 NASB).

Too many unmarried couples lie to themselves, thinking if they withhold intercourse, they can engage in all kinds of other sexual activity, including oral sex, fondling, and sexual play in many forms. Ephesians 5:3 makes it abundantly clear, "Among you there must not be even a hint of sexual immorality or any kind of impurity . . . because these are improper for God's holy people."

Sexual Loss

When our spouse dies, so does our sex life. As we sat around my living room the day I buried Brian, I listened to some of my relatives joke about sex. I wanted to scream, "How insensitive of you! I just buried my sexual partner, and you jest about it in my presence?"

Mitchell felt terribly guilty about sexual twinges he experienced as he hugged women on the day of his wife's funeral. Thankfully, he read later that our bodies sometimes respond this way after loss. Imagine the guilt and confusion if no one explains normalcy!

Amazingly, many people, including Christians, become sexually active soon after losing their spouse. According to our study of the Bible, sex in any form outside of marriage qualifies as sin.

Even non-Christian counselors will tell you it's not emotionally healthy to engage in promiscuous behavior, especially soon after the loss of a spouse. We become one with sexual partners. Extramarital sex causes more grief and confusion.

So what do we do about our sexual urges?

Answers

No clear-cut answers exist as to how one should manage sexual desires in the midst of grief. I found only two books that even discussed the subject. One author, a Christian psychologist, states "Meeting your sexual needs without a partner is, without a doubt, one of the most difficult issues surviving spouses face, and it may add frustration and sadness to your loss."[27] He advocates self-pleasuring (masturbation) as a viable option. An article from Focus on the Family, however, considers this option sin.[28]

Sin?

As to the question of sin? I googled "Christianity and masturbation" and found some thought-provoking material. Certainly, the Bible says nothing on the topic of "self-pleasuring." What it does say? "Everyone who looks on a woman to lust for her has committed adultery with her already in his heart" (Matt. 5:27–28). Scripture makes it clear. It's not okay to lust after someone other than your spouse. It is, therefore, not okay to masturbate while lusting after someone else, a picture (pornography), or anything other than your own spouse.

But I can't consider reliving memories with your love as sinful. Your sexual relationship within your marriage qualified as biblical and beautiful in God's eyes. Obsessing over your sexual experience with your spouse, however, may qualify as unhealthy. And, obviously at some point—especially if we desire to remarry—we must purpose not to dwell on past memories in order to move forward.

The apostle Paul wrote, "It is God's will that you should be sanctified; that you should avoid sexual immorality; that each of you should learn to control your own body in a way that is holy and honorable, not in passionate lust like the pagans, who do not know God" (1 Thess. 4:3–5).

The bottom line? God calls us to live a holy life, which includes the following:

- A holy thought life
- Holy behavior
- Holy sexuality

I recommend you do some research, including the following articles, and ask God to give you wisdom and clarity in this matter:

- www.acts17-11.com/dialogsmasturbation.html
- www.carm.org/masturbation.[29]

Memories

As widows, we naturally replay wonderful memories of intimate times with our spouse. Married couples share intimacy and often refer to special times together. How, then, can they put those thoughts out of their minds just because one of them died?

I see nothing wrong with reliving those times as a way of remembering your spouse. Chip indicated at one point the only thing he could remember about his wife was their intimate moments. By recreating some of his favorite moments with her in his mind, he could remember her. I can't condemn him for that.

Some widows wake up in the night dreaming of sexual experiences with their deceased spouse. Wet dreams happen. We certainly can't control our dreams, and God himself deems the intimacy we shared within our marriage as good.

Be holy, for I am holy.

Leviticus 10:3, 11:44, 45

May your spirit, soul, and body be kept blameless at the coming of our Lord Jesus Christ.

1 Thessalonians 5:23

Flee from sexual immorality. All other sins a person commits are outside the body, but whoever sins sexually, sins against their own body.

1 Corinthians 6:18

REVEL IN THE GOOD DAYS

"Just as tears give vent to the deep sorrow we feel, laughter reveals that while grief may have a grip on us, it hasn't choked the life out of us. . . . It gives us a mini-vacation from our pain."

~Nancy Guthrie

"In good times, laughter comes easily, feels natural and taken for granted. In grief, it is a difficult task," I wrote in my journal. Yet I remember times when the ability to laugh surprised me. Most days felt nauseatingly painful, and I wondered if I would ever know happiness again. When laughter erupted, it came as a welcome gift.

Experiencing happiness, even for a few minutes, buries some people deep in a canyon of guilt. I say revel in the good days and moments because they occur rarely. Death sucks the life out of us, so enjoy every good moment. Savor them. It does our body good.

Laughter

Laughter amps up our body's production of endorphins, a natural painkiller.[30] Don't fear—or avoid—laughter because laughter and joy can keep you hanging on for better days. Laughter doesn't mean you no longer miss your loved one. It simply means you found a ray of sunshine in the dark abyss.

After her husband's funeral, LaTanya quietly whispered to me her confession—she felt guilty for enjoying some shopping. At that point, though she was still in shock, I told her not to worry. She should enjoy what she could because she would have plenty days ahead that would steal her fun.

Laughter & Tears

Do not take this to mean we should not cry or strive for happiness all the time. My point? If you happen upon a good day and find yourself able to laugh, revel in it. It is healthy to "cry a Mississippi,"[31] as well as to laugh.

During Brian's illness I regularly sent e-mails to numerous friends and family with updates on Brian's condition. A year after his death, I sent an e-mail telling of *our* condition:

> We managed by God's grace to make it through almost one whole year without Brian. It's been extremely difficult, but we are amazed and grateful that we managed to keep going. We find ourselves able to laugh and cry, sometimes all in the same sentence.

> Laughter and tears can, and do, coexist. Take advantage of your good days, and do something productive or fun. You deserve a few good moments.

> A cheerful heart is good *medicine*, but a crushed spirit dries up the bones.
>
> Proverbs 17:22 (*emphasis mine*)

SORTING/CLEANING OUT

"I couldn't face another empty half. I already had so many: his side of the car, his side of the bed, his chair at the table, his end of the couch, his place in the pew, his voice on the other end of the phone . . . so I avoided removing his clothes from his side of [the] closet."

~Lois Mowday Rabey

Simply thinking about having to sort through our spouse's things can overwhelm us. Actually accomplishing the task, even more so. My number one piece of advice, especially early on: *Your choice. Your terms.*

Some people want to tackle the job immediately and get it over with, while others hang on to things for years. Eventually, we all have to face the sorting process. Some things we simply must part with, while we can cherish others for a lifetime.

Elderly

Adult children often encourage their elderly parents to clean out when they can conveniently help. While perfectly understandable, especially if the children don't live nearby, you have every right to fall apart and tell them you simply cannot handle it at this point. A suggested compromise in this situation: you choose a few things that give you comfort and bring special memories. Your children may then clean out the rest of the closet as they see fit.

A Note to Family and Friends

I cannot say this strongly enough: You can't comprehend the amount of pain you cause by forcing someone to remove their loved one's belongings. When ripped from the body of their love, people naturally cling to things that represent them. What may seem trite or sensible to you can push a grieving person over the edge. Some people handle this logically and may even need or want things cleaned out and removed. Others can't bear it. Be patient with your friend, parent, or family member. Your job? To love them through this, not boss them through it.

Little by Little

If you can't face the whole "cleaning out" task, consider doing a little at a time. No one, for instance, will likely want to use your spouse's underwear. Start with that drawer. A friend or family member can take care of that task while you are away from the house or away from the bedroom. Keep chipping away at it a little at a time as you can handle it.

As you clean out, consider allowing family members and close friends to choose items that mean something to them. Some will cherish items that belonged to your love while others find it too hard. Try not to take their choices personally.

Charitable Clothing

Often a natural reason arises to give away certain things. About six months after Brian died, we met a young hospital worker from Kenya who studied in the United States. He appeared close to Brian's size, and I discovered one day that he didn't own a winter coat. He couldn't afford one. I could not have lived with myself had I not shared with him a perfectly good coat that hung unused in the closet. It gave my kids a sense of pride to help someone in need. We included a few additional items of warm clothing in case he needed them too. He was ecstatic!

Later in the year, our church planned a garage sale to raise money for summer missions. I didn't think I could handle seeing men at church in Brian's shirts, so I donated clothing I wouldn't recognize—mostly dress pants and jeans.

Ten years after his death, Cara keeps her dad's clothes exactly where they hung in his closet when he died. Think about that. After ten years the clothing styles change, and they smell musty. Dry rot sets in, and leaving them in the closet for ten years doesn't bring her dad back.

In most of the surveys I took, people gave the clothes to charity. It gave them a sense of satisfaction to help someone in need. At least for a while, I think it's perfectly fine to hold on to a few items of clothing that hold special meaning to you.

Precious Memorials

At one juncture it became a matter of survival for me. I saw the train wreck coming. I knew if I didn't clean out the closet and find a way to accept my single status, I wouldn't make it. My children, however, couldn't bear to let go of their dad's shirts that defined his wardrobe to them. Some sweet ladies in our church offered to make throw quilts for the kids out of Brian's shirts. They now hold memories of his clothing in the form of blankets to keep them warm. What a wonderful gift.

If you would like to do something like this, I found a website that specializes in this very thing: www.recover-from-grief.com/comfort-and-sympathy.html.

Time Frame

Recommendations on the matter of cleaning out the closet differ quite radically. At some point it becomes detrimental to your emotional health to hang on to everything. I wouldn't put a hard and fast rule on it, but certainly by the end of the second year, I recommend you part with most of the clothing and personal items. Others recommend as early as the first six months.[32] Keep in mind, too, that the process of cleaning out forces us to keep moving forward.

Gifts

For the first couple of Christmases after Brian's death, I selected some items that belonged to their dad to give to our kids as gifts from him. These were things I didn't need to hang onto myself, but the kids enjoyed. I gave Brian's watch to one of the boys and his special chess set to our daughter who enjoyed playing the game with him. His cowboy hat went to the child who collects hats. I also gave Brian's mom the sweater she knitted for him, and his dad received his expensive pen.

Although Nikki may not have played the game since Brian's death, she cherishes the chess set as a special memory of the games they shared. In no form or fashion does AJ portray the cowboy, but he proudly displays his dad's hat on his wall.

The kids also decided they'd each like a pillow made from one of their dad's shirts. To me, it feels a little eerie, and I find it too painful to put my arms around them. But they find comfort in lounging on a cushion that reminds them of their dad. Mind you, eventually these pillows get a little dirty, and at some point they will have to part with them or clean them, but for a time the pillows can bring solace to their aching souls.

Beyond the Clothing

Each widow must eventually deal with the tedious task of sorting all of the papers, files, knick-knacks, tools, and more. Since there's no easy way to tackle this job, just put on your working hat and get to it. If it helps, invite a compassionate friend or relative to join you. Howard's friend, Diane, challenged him to get rid of anything he didn't think he would use. It became a joke with his kids that if they couldn't find it, "Diane must have gotten rid of it."

Heirlooms

Tough decisions arise regarding heirlooms, especially if and when you remarry. The question? What to do with two households full of furniture? Small children may not feel emotionally attached to family pieces, and yet the obligation still exists to pass heirlooms down through the family of origin. Older children may want you to save everything for them. Both Howard's family and mine had emotional attachments, as well as family heirlooms. One home could not accommodate all the children as well as all of the stuff, though.

Let me say, here: *All family heirlooms must pass through the DNA line!* I've heard too many horror stories where new step-parents take family heirlooms and pass them down through their own family line, leaving the DNA family nothing of their own mother or dad's belongings. No matter how you want to justify it, this is wrong.

We chose to part with things that wouldn't last and stored others for the kids. We rented two storage units for a couple of years until the kids started moving out. We chose to make the financial sacrifice temporarily. Not everyone can do that, however.

Howard and I both retain attachments to things belonging and pertaining to our first spouse. Please remember, in no way does this indicate lack of love or appreciation for the new spouse. If you find yourself struggling with jealousy or the inability to support his attachment to his first wife's belongings, understand it has nothing to do with you. Talk about your feelings and discuss a balance.

If he wants to hang on to her lingerie, I think that qualifies as a problem. If he loves a particular picture of her, no problem. Howard and I both keep pictures of each other, as well as Brian and Ann in our offices—and all around the house. Maybe we're strange, but Brian's death and Ann's death don't take away our love for them. In the same way we love many children, we maintain the capacity to love each other in addition to our first spouses.

And, just to make you feel better, although remarried for four years at this writing, we still haven't accomplished the task of sorting through all of the boxes! We will deal with this overwhelming, time-consuming, and emotional ordeal when time allows—or maybe once the items start to disintegrate!

Personal Items

I surprise myself how attached I still find myself to clothing and other gifts Brian gave me. Recently I cleaned out my closet. I came across a suit Brian bought me before my first pregnancy. Though still beautiful, it's horribly out of style. At the time of this writing, my first child just turned twenty-four years old, which makes the suit almost twenty-five years old. Get the picture?

At the time it looked expensive and regal, such a sweet gift from Brian. But I probably wore the suit only once in the last ten years. Definitely time to say good-bye. But the sweet gesture the suit represents makes it hard to part with. Even as I write this, I find myself tempted to pull it out of the giveaway bag. Someone had better remove it from the house quickly, before I change my mind!

My mother totaled her car in an accident a year or two after my dad died. He specifically purchased the car for her, thinking he might not live long. He wanted her to have a nice, reliable car. With the insurance money, Mom purchased a newer version of the exact car Dad bought her. Most people get excited for any reason to buy a new car. Instead, Mom grieved the loss of the older one Dad so thoughtfully provided. Eventually she could reconcile God's miraculous provision of a car that would last even longer, and she expressed gratitude. But it didn't take away the grief she felt over the one that held her love's fingerprints.

Sadie finds it both weird and pleasing when her dad wears some of her deceased husband's shoes, which he asked permission to do. Her dad will never buy himself nice shoes. The fact that he wears several of her husband's shoes gives her comfort.

While our feelings may not be rational, they most certainly are normal. Sometimes we must allow ourselves to grieve while reminding ourselves that these are only things—earthly possessions. It's okay to feel irrational while forcing ourselves to accomplish the rational.

NUGGETS OF GRACE

"I can honestly say that out of the deepest pain has come the strongest conviction of the presence of God and the love of God."

~ Elizabeth Elliot

There are always blessings in the storm. Don't miss them. Karl and Nancy asked how we managed to survive the craziness that comes with cancer permeating our daily lives. I relayed many stories of the misery of cancer, and then disclosed that I can't talk about the difficulties without also mentioning the blessings. In the midst of trial, God always shows up.

I told them how others reached out to help us. How God showed up in small ways, as well as in big ones. An airline pilot in our church donated free airline miles for us to use when traveling to Houston to the cancer center. Friends chipped in to help fund the $5,000 chemo treatments which insurance didn't cover. Checks arrived in the mail—sometimes from relative strangers—just when we needed money most.

Mercy in the Mundane

Even when Brian died, I could see small nuggets of God's goodness. Eventually I understood that just the ability to get up every morning and take my children to school qualified as a blessing. Some days I could actually laugh. What a blessing! My family and a few close friends stuck by me. I could call any one of them at any time, pour out my heart, and receive comfort. They could not carry my burden, but they helped to support me through it.

When June fought suicidal temptations, a friend who understood showed up because he recognized the signs. June and Ethan became best friends as they shared the experience of grief. Although they dated for a while, she couldn't commit to a long-term relationship with him. She wondered how to find God in all of the craziness. I pointed out that God sent Ethan when she needed help. Even if he was intended as a short-lived gift, he exemplified an enormous nugget of God's grace in her dark world. His presence literally saved her life.

The Thirty-Five Year Plan

Two months after Brian's death I kept thinking about a book I read as a child. I didn't remember the details of the book, but I knew it changed my life. I felt compelled to find this book called *Not My Will*.

I purchased the book online and devoured it in one day after it arrived. I sat in my bed weeping as the realization of God's amazing grace to me sank in. I knew it for sure.

God himself placed this book in my hands a full thirty-five years earlier to prepare me for this day. How could I not fall down and worship him for loving me that much? If God could put a book into my hands on a remote island of Indonesia three and a half decades before I needed it, I could trust him to care for my wounded soul.

Write 'Em Down

It's a good exercise to list all of the negatives in our lives. Writing them down helps us to recognize the causes for our pain. It opens our eyes to the depth of our suffering and allows us to afford ourselves some grace.

Soon after Brian's diagnosis, a counselor challenged me to write down everything I found difficult in my life. After three pages, I began to understand. Three pages of troubles gave me perspective. Seeing it in writing didn't take it away, but it helped me comprehend the magnitude of my suffering.

After identifying the negatives, list the positives. Losing our spouse is one of the most difficult things we will ever face. We need to feel the pain and allow ourselves to grieve. We must also force ourselves to look at the positives. The positives serve as nuggets of hope. They provide us with reasons to keep going.

We can cling to hope when we see the good things that take place in the middle of our mess. The nuggets of hope encourage us to keep hanging on even when we don't *feel* God's presence. Positives prove God's goodness, whether or not we *feel* it, and serve as a beacon of hope.

> Every good and perfect gift comes from above, coming down from the Father of the heavenly lights, who does not change like shifting shadows.
>
> *James 1:17*

HOPE

"Of one thing I am perfectly sure: God's story never ends with ashes."
~Elizabeth Elliot, These Strange Ashes

Where do we find hope? *Can* we find hope? Hope may be the one thing we widows need most. So many of us lose hope. The loss of our spouse and best friend fills us with hopelessness, which then leads to depression.

After Brian's initial diagnosis, people in my life tried to encourage me with empty words. I found none of their efforts encouraging. Finally, I snapped and honestly told my friend her words did not bring encouragement.

"What encourages you?" She asked.

"The only thing is the hope I have that God will see me through."

My Hope

Truly, my only hope rested in the character and trustworthiness of my Heavenly Father. I met with Vera, whose husband also battled brain cancer. She didn't want to hear about God. I didn't know how to help her without bringing God into it. Through it all, he remains my only hope. Without God, I could claim no hope whatsoever.

This may sound like rubbish to you. I write from experience, however. We cannot count on people, doctors, friends, or family to save us from our sorrow. Nor can they bring our spouses back from the grave. The only person to ever conquer the grave is Jesus Christ, and scripture tells us the final enemy to see defeat is death.

> What does not last will be dressed with what lasts forever. What dies will be dressed with what does not die. Then what is written will come true. It says, "Death has been swallowed up. It has lost the battle"
>
> *1 Corinthians 15:54, NIrV*

Therein lies my hope.

Resurrection Reunions

In his book, *Honest Wrestling*, my husband Howard addresses the question of hope in two chapters. He explains the coming resurrection of believers who died on earth, reunion with their bodies, and everlasting life on the New Earth.

> Resurrection is no longer an essential doctrine for me to believe. Resurrection is my anchor. It defines my future. It's everything I'm banking on. It's why I haven't quit. Resurrection will give us strong, young, healthy bodies. . . . Our minds will always be sharp and our motives always pure. We will have intimacy only dreamed of in this life, with relationships never marred by selfishness or destroyed by separation. We will have unending time to enjoy old friends and make new ones, to remember joys and trials from our present life, and to create new adventures in the next one. We will serve and honor Jesus Christ in perfect obedience, never again tempted to sin. We will have life as God originally intended and long ago promised. And this real, physical, and truly human life will never end.[33]

Our ultimate goal: inhabiting The New Earth. In essence, if we (and our spouse) know Jesus Christ as our Lord and Savior, we can count on a blessed reunion on the New Earth. Although our marriage relationship won't continue, Howard believes we will know each other and remember our earthly union. Clearly I can't continue a marriage relationship with both Howard and Brian in eternity, but possibly we will all be close friends.

The Bible says we do not have to grieve in the same way as those who have no hope (1 Thess. 4:13) because we will see our loved ones again.

> "Our resurrection hope reaches into the grave and overwhelms the devastation of death. Resurrection will restore what was amputated, compensate for all that was stolen, and reverse the irreversible."[34]

Therein lies hope.

Key to Hope

How can we find this hope? The Bible tells us to "Believe in the Lord Jesus, and you will be saved—you and your household" (Acts 16:31).

What exactly does that mean?

- In the very beginning God created a perfect world, which he declared to be "very good" (Gen. 1:1, 1:31).

- The humans he placed in this perfect world wanted to be like God and were tricked (by the evil one) into believing it was possible to be like God. Instead of trusting God's good character, they believed a lie and chose to disobey. In that instant sin entered the world and separated us from God (Gen. 2:4–3:24).

- God loves every human. "For God so loved the world that he gave his one and only Son, that whoever believes in him shall not perish but have eternal life" (John 3:16).

- We need to recognize ourselves as sinners, separated from God. "For *all* have sinned and fall short of the glory of God," (Rom. 3:23). "For the wages of sin is death, but the *gift* of God is *eternal life* in Jesus Christ our Lord" (Rom. 6:23, emphasis mine).

- God provided a way to redeem the separation between God and man by sending his son, Jesus, to die on a cross. By dying, he paid the price for all of our sins. He was buried and rose again on the third day, defeating death and sin. "But God demonstrates his own love for us in this: While we were still sinners, Christ died for us" (Rom. 5:8).

- We can accept and trust Jesus as the One who gives us the gift of hope. "For it is by grace you have been saved through faith—and this not from yourselves, it is the *gift* of God—not by works, so that no one can boast" (Eph. 2:8–9, emphasis mine).

How to Accept the Gift of Hope

The only requirement is that we believe:

- God created and loves us.
- We live as sinners.
- Jesus died for our sins.
- Jesus is the One who gives us the gift of hope.

We can pray and thank him for loving us, apologize for our sin, acknowledge that we sin regularly, and then ask him to take over our life and give us hope. A simple prayer of repentance and acceptance places us into the family of God.

Where is Hope?

Our only hope lies in *trusting* Jesus Christ, the One who himself died to pay the price for our sin, offering hope for now and hope for our future. Our suffering will pale in the face of an eternal union with Christ himself. All will one day be restored.

Therein lies hope.

If you want more information about how you can trust in this Jesus, contact info@abhbooks.com.

See also "Jesus' Example" under my "Emotional Support" section.

Part Three

WHEN DEATH NO LONGER WINS

MOVING FORWARD

"Inside your soul is the ability to survive even the toughest storms, and that paradise can always be found—even in the middle of a hurricane—if you are willing to look."

~ Denise Hildreth Jones

"When are you going to move on? Don't you think it's time for you to move on?" How many times have we heard questions similar to these? I hate the words, "Move on" and refuse to use them.

How can someone ask me to "move on" from the one I loved and lived with for nineteen years? I will never stop loving Brian. He was my best friend for twenty years. We parented three children together. We fought the enemy of cancer together. We laughed and cried together. We shared a faith that gave us hope.

Moving On

I know our friends mean we need to find a life of some sort beyond the grief when they tell us to "move on." I know what they mean. They want us to find happiness. They tire of our pain and sadness. They really do mean well, but they don't know what it's like to lose their best friend and lover. They can't comprehend what it means to "move on."

Most widows don't *want* to move on. We don't *want* to forget. We *want* to hang on to our memories and keep the memory of our loved one alive. And then our friends tell us to "move on." It's infuriating, to say the least.

Moving Forward

Yes, at some point we need to find a way to happiness. We need to make a new life for ourselves. But we will carry the grief with us. The power of grief diminishes over time, but it never fully goes away. We learn to live with the mix of joy and sorrow.

At this point in my life, I feel happy on most days. I find great joy in my new life. But days still sneak up on me when the grief overwhelms and I feel completely hopeless. Sometimes I actually feel panic that I can't live without Brian, even though I've already lived many years without him. Brian's birthday, the anniversary of the day he died, and our wedding anniversary continue to render me useless. I tire of the grief when it hits, and I wish I *could* "get over it" and "move on."

Even now, four years into my wonderful, new marriage, and down to only one teen at home, we often catch ourselves "knocked to the mat," as my husband, Howard, says. Although it should no longer surprise me, grief continually attacks as a burglar in the night.

I tell people if they don't understand the Facebook posts and tweets from those whom they feel should have moved on by now, hear this. We don't move on. We move forward.

We adapt to a new, different life. We learn to enjoy the "new normal." We appreciate the new gifts God gives us. We find happiness again. But the love, life, and memories we shared with the dead don't just go away because they left this earth.

We keep living, but we continue to miss our loved ones on holidays, on their birthdays, and on just any ol' day in which their memory takes our breath away.

James Means, remarried for twenty-five years after his first wife died, proves this: "I found great happiness in remarriage. She surely is God's precious and beautiful gift . . . [however] there remains a deep reservoir of hurt . . . Real wounds of the soul never heal in this life."[1]

> The righteous keep moving forward, and those with clean hands become stronger and stronger.
>
> *Job 17:9 NLT*

GET BACK ON THE HORSE

"Tell me, what is it you plan to do with your one wild and precious life?"

~ Mary Oliver

About eighteen months into my grief, darkness consumed me. I could barely function. In addition to antidepressants (I don't mind admitting), I constantly sought the Lord for help. I journaled:

> Lord, you are my Rock and my Shield, my Fortress. You will not allow my feet to stumble. You will be the defender of the widow and a father to my fatherless children. You will give grace; you will give comfort; you will give wisdom; you will give strength. In my weakness you are strong.
>
> God is not only good when he takes away the pain, but he is also good in the midst of it.
>
> I am weary of being sad. I forgot how to have fun. I need to take some purposeful steps toward making sure I have some fun.

I realized I had two choices: crater completely or claw my way out of the darkness. Although newly single, I still felt married. I needed to find a way to accept my plight of singleness, so I made four conscious, strategic decisions: pry wedding rings off, purge the closet of Brian's clothes, exercise, and make the effort to have some fun.

Positive Choices

When we recognize our inability to function, and find ourselves spiraling downward, we need to do something about it. Although I took antidepressants, deeper depression threatened to swallow me. A counselor suggested I go see my doctor. The doctor changed my prescription, indicating that sometimes our bodies adjust to an antidepressant over a period of time, requiring a change. The change made a huge difference, but I still had to make proactive choices.

I removed my wedding rings on March 9, 2010. What a monumental day! I felt both freedom and enormous grief. Excitement that I might actually find hope, but grief over the fact that my life would forever change. My kids grieved as well, though they all agreed I needed to do what it took to move forward.

As mentioned, a few ladies in our church offered to make throw blankets for my kids out of Brian's shirts. This prompted me to remove the clothes from the closet and provided sweet mementos for the kids.

I met a friend once a week to walk. We pounded the floor with our feet, while pouring out our hearts over the issues of life. I also purchased exercise bands and created a ten-minute workout routine. I began to feel more energetic and proud that I'd accomplished something. I wanted to call Brian and tell him of my successes. This brought more grief.

The kids and I joined a group of friends who line danced. Although vastly out of my comfort zone, I enjoyed laughing and creating some fun. We went camping with our friends, along with a bunch of teenagers, and had a blast. With every forward move, I experienced more grief because I couldn't tell Brian of my progress. With time, however, the space between bouts of tears lengthened. I no longer cried *every* day, although I continued to experience great loneliness.

Create a New Life

Creating a new life may mean something completely different to each person. We all recognize our lives have changed, but we don't like it. Finding a way to reinvent ourselves signifies progress toward healing. We no longer exist as two. We must uncover the key to living as one.

On the one hand, this can bring exhilaration. On the other hand, we grieve the reason for the necessary changes. I decided the time had come for me to go back to work. With this decision came both excitement and sadness. I looked forward to doing something I always wanted to do by working for a missions organization. I worried, however, how this change would affect my children.

Again, two steps forward, one step back. Even one step back represents progress, as it doesn't take us all the way back. Moving forward takes drive, planning, effort, and sheer determination. We may still fall on our faces in a puddle of tears over and over again during the process, however.

I can do all this through him [Christ] who gives me strength.

Philippians 4:13

DATING

"It is wonderful to feel alive again. Your emotions zing all over the place, and your reason may take an extended vacation."

~Lois Mowday Rabey

I received a greeting card from a friend that read, "The only thing worse than being alone is a blind date." Oh, how true that statement felt, and I laughed out loud!

If you've read this far, I expect the notion at least intrigues you. Whether you can't stomach the idea of dating again, or eagerly anticipate it, the fact remains that dating is now an option for you.

Confusion

The thought of dating again literally nauseated me the first year and a half after Brian's death. I spent the next six months in a state of emotional confusion. Feeling so terribly alone made me want to consider dating, but merely thinking about it threw me into tears and another cycle of grief.

The first time I found myself attracted to another man, I totally freaked out. While I still wore my wedding rings, I found myself drawn to a handsome, single man. As I examined my feelings for Leroy, I realized the attraction occurred because he reminded me of Brian—big, tall, teddy bear sort, who seemed kind and fun.

We developed a friendship, and a few months later he offered to help with a project at my house. Excited yet frightened, I accepted his offer but foolishly inquired as to his intentions. I couldn't afford to play games. My children needed to know what to expect. *I* needed to know what to expect. I thanked him for being kind since others who came to help hadn't always acted so kindly, and I cried. Every time I thought about Leroy's kindness, I cried. My heart wrenched in so many pieces.

Excitement came over the idea of experiencing a relationship with a man again, but sadness stole my joy because spending time with another man meant Brian was truly gone. It grieved me deeply. I realized dating and new relationships would require much more of me emotionally this time around. Grief now tagged along, and the emotions attached created a mess.

The Right Time

No one can really tell us when the time comes to date. I witness the gamut when observing others and dating time frames. I know some who married within the first year, although they admit now they probably wouldn't recommend it. I know others who waited ten or fifteen years before remarrying, though most of those dated much sooner. They tended to encounter lots of frustration in the dating arena.

Most professional counselors recommend waiting at least two years before dating. The first two years after our spouse's death command too much of us emotionally.

Some actually begin dating in order to avoid the pain of grief. This option typically adds to the grief rather than masking it, and doing so drags the new partner into the mix. Many second marriages end because the widow didn't deal with his or her pain first.

As I state in my chapter, "Don't Be Stupid," author and counselor, Gary Smalley believes, "Any new romantic relationship that comes within two years of the death of a spouse or divorce will most likely lead to additional pain, conflict and heart damage."[2]

Pressure

As I said before, pressure to date usually comes as an unwelcome conversation. Well-meaning friends should stay out of our business in this area, unless we ask them to join in. They want us to be happy, and they assume remarriage will fix this problem of sadness that hangs around our necks. They don't think through the ramifications of their plea, nor do they understand that forcing us into dating only creates more anxiety, grief, and pain.

We can't throw off the grief and "move on." How I wish that were possible! It takes time to work through our grief. It takes time to find another good fit as well. We can't just snap our fingers and voila! There's the perfect person to sweep us off our feet and fix everything. Dating and remarriage require work, which some of us can't yet take on.

My friend, Janice had the opposite experience. She started dating in the second year after her husband's suicide. She felt terribly alone and needed companionship, but her friends couldn't understand. They put pressure on her *not* to date.

Either way, friends often put unwanted pressure on us when they haven't a clue what we live with on a daily basis. As I said before, I finally told one friend I simply couldn't date yet. "I'm going to be sad for a while. I need you to be okay with that." Feel free to gently tell your well-meaning friends to back off.

"Letting Go"

For me, "letting go" was the hardest part. I constantly questioned in my journal what it means to "let go," and how one manages to accomplish it. While, on the one hand, it would seem obvious and easy, I couldn't let go because I didn't *want* to let go. I wanted the freedom to keep loving Brian and love someone else, too, but I assumed that option didn't exist.

One night, Leroy indicated his impression that women don't need men anymore. They can take their own car to the shop or hire a handyman. Because Brian fought illness for so long, he couldn't do the "man jobs" around our house, but I needed his friendship, emotional support, wisdom, and so much more.

I found myself incensed over Leroy's statement and began creating a list of reasons why I believe women need men. Why *I* needed *my* man. Before I knew it I listed more than sixty reasons I needed Brian. Why I need a man. At that moment it dawned on me: I want all of those things again. I want to love someone who can love me back.

I finally realized I could keep loving Brian but open my heart to add another love, just like we do when we add a child to the family. Before my second child came, I worried that I couldn't love two children. How foolish of me! I adored him just as much as I did the first one.

The trick, here, is finding someone who can live with this dichotomy. Finding such a person requires dating and marrying a person whose confidence in us and the new relationship nullifies the threat of the dead spouse. This person allows us the freedom to continue loving our deceased spouse.

I knew I found a winner when Howard encouraged me to continue wearing the ring Brian gave me for our 15th wedding anniversary. I wear it to this day and will continue to do so unless one of my boys decides to marry and chooses this ring for his bride. Howard gifted me with permission to continue my love for Brian, while loving him, too. Please don't settle for someone who can't allow you this privilege. It will always bring tension to your relationship.

Dating Websites

I know only a few people who found healthy love on dating websites. I know numerous people for whom doing so ended tragically. Honestly, I am not a proponent of dating websites for these reasons:

- How do you know if you're getting the truth?
- It's difficult to check out their stories.
- No one can vouch for their history or character.
- Digging into someone's background requires much energy.
- You meet a ton of frogs in the process of looking for a prince.
- I watch many get their hopes up and then their hearts broken.

That said, I would not necessarily tell you to stay away from dating sites completely. I do encourage you, however, to act with great caution. I cannot say I would never have joined a dating website, because I don't know how I would've felt after a long period of singleness. I do understand the deep longing for love and the loneliness that accompanies widowhood. Just please be careful!

Good Old-Fashioned Advice

Whether meeting people on a dating site or dating people you know, I share my advice from experience and observation. And even though it may seem like advice for women, men should also take heed to the same bits of caution.

- Be careful and wise. I cannot stress this enough.
- Meet people in safe, public places.
- Do not give anyone your home address under any circumstances until you know their character and trustworthiness. The last thing you need is a stalker who knows where to find you.
- Conduct a background check no matter what. If the person balks, too bad. They don't get to date you.

- Build a friendship before jumping into a dating relationship.

- Know what characteristics you need and desire before dating.

- Stick to your own standards.

- Do *not* settle. Janna regularly picks guys with bad track records. If you choose to date an alcoholic, you get an alcoholic, no matter how nice he appears. Nothing positive can come out of that. Please don't give in to desperation and settle for trouble.

- Believe you deserve the best, and hold out for a wonderful person.

- Do *not* enter into a sexual relationship outside of marriage. No matter what you believe biblically, sex outside of marriage confuses your emotions and makes your situation much worse. Entering into a sexual relationship before marriage breaks all trust. Bottom line: if he willingly sleeps with you before marriage, he may sleep with others once he marries you. A willingness to wait gives credence to trust.

- Yes, you *can* wait to engage in sexual activity. It's not easy, but it's possible. I *do* understand. I made it.

- Set boundaries to protect yourself.

Red Flags
Watch out for potential dates who do the following:

- Don't agree with you spiritually.

- Pressure you to "move on."

- Show jealousy toward your late spouse.

- Don't allow you to talk about your late spouse.

- Ignore your children.

- Talk only about themselves.

- Pressure you in any way.

- Make you feel sad.

- Treat you poorly.

- Put their own needs above yours.

Green Lights

Cautiously proceed with someone who:

- Loves the Lord and challenges you spiritually.
- Gives you permission to talk about and still love your late spouse.
- Respects you and your needs.
- Genuinely finds you and your story interesting.
- Cares about your children.
- Holds you accountable to your own convictions.
- Cherishes and adores you.
- Puts your needs above his own.
- Brings joy and happiness to your world.

Do *not* allow yourself to settle for less.

Healthy Places to Meet Someone New

Choose to spend your time in places where emotionally healthy people tend to hang out. I realize I can promise no guarantees, because unhealthy people hang out everywhere, but the better places to meet people include: at church, in a volunteer setting, at a friend's home or event, at a dog park, and at restaurants.

Unhealthy Places to Meet

Healthy, lasting relationships rarely begin in bars, night clubs, adult video stores, and the like.

Comparisons

Comparisons happen naturally. We can't help but notice differences in our late spouse and a new person in our lives. On the positive side, comparisons help evaluate a person's actions and character. If you can enjoy Brad's character and personality, while appreciating and recognizing the differences, he may qualify as a good dating partner.

If, on the other hand, you find yourself constantly comparing the differences and not enjoying Joe (or Josephine) for his unique qualities, either he is not right for you, or you aren't yet ready to date.

Questions to Ask Yourself

Sandra began dating a widower about a year and a half after her husband died. She asked me if she should continue dating Nate, as she found herself constantly thinking about her husband, Jack. I suggested she ask herself some pertinent questions in order to better evaluate the situation:

- Do you *always* think about Jack even when you're with Nate, or do you just talk about him with Nate in between other enjoyable conversations?

- Can you enjoy Nate as an individual, albeit a different one from Jack?

- Do you get excited or giddy about spending time with Nate? Or do you spend time with him to keep from feeling alone?

- Do you and Nate have enough in common that you could see yourself *loving* life with him?

- What do you like about Nate? Is he just a warm body, or do you love who he is as a person?

Do not be yoked together with unbelievers. For what do righteousness and wickedness have in common? Or what fellowship can light have with darkness?

2 Corinthians 6:14

REMARRIAGE?

"I have found great happiness in remarriage. She surely is God's precious and beautiful gift [yet] there remains a deep reservoir of hurt that is mostly hidden from my family and friends. Real wounds of the soul never heal in this life."

~James Means

Remarriage can bring great joy, as well as great sorrow. We absolutely cannot enter into a second marriage with our eyes closed, especially when children constitute part of the equation. I would do it all over again, but the task of putting two families together can destroy a couple if they don't enter in with all the gusto they can muster. Honestly, I sometimes marvel that we made it through those first years.

"Integrating a stepfamily is one of the most difficult tasks for any family in America today," says Ron Deal, author of *The Smart Stepfamily*.[3]

Again, this topic could fill an entire book, so I will try to address only the basics.

What Scripture Says

In 1 Corinthians 7:1–9, Paul highly recommends widows remain unmarried in order to give themselves to ministry. When involved in ministry, a person can stay focused and not worry about the distractions of family and spouse. I assume Paul means those widows who don't have the charge of children at home. If the widow burns with sexual passion, however (1 Cor. 7:9), and can't focus on ministry, Paul endorses marriage.

First Timothy 5:3–16 gives direction to the church with regard to widows in need. For the most part, Timothy places the obligation on extended family to care for their needy widows. If the church must take on the responsibility of widows, he provides guidelines. Within those parameters, his suggestion for older widows (over sixty): that they participate in "good deeds" of service in order to receive help from the church. Timothy advises younger widows to remarry, as "their sensual desires overcome their dedication to Christ" (v. 11). His experience apparently tells him they tend toward becoming idle, gossips, and busybodies (v. 13).

Keep in mind, these are *recommendations*. It appears widows may choose their own direction, as each widow will encounter different needs, passions, and desires.

Absolute Necessities

I never agreed with legal documents like pre-nuptial agreements until Brian died and I considered remarriage. I fully believe we should go into marriage planning to make it. If we don't, we enter into marriage foolishly. But reality and experience tell us not all marriages make it. We must act wisely, especially when money and/or children fill the picture. Blending stepfamilies proves extremely challenging and, according to Ron Deal, 60-65 percent of remarriages that include children end in divorce within the first five years.[4]

If one partner going into the marriage has acquired significantly more financial resources than the other, it makes sense to sign a pre-nuptial agreement. I hear more stories of people getting married and then one of them goes nuts. We need to plan for the outside chance that we picked one of those nuts—just in case. Con men (and women) do exist, and they love to find rich widows, sweep them off their feet, take all they own, and then leave them. We owe it to our late husband or wife to protect what they left us, if for no other reason than for our children. A person willing to sign a pre-nup can usually be trusted, but beware just the same.

Redoing your will becomes another necessity when choosing to remarry. Please don't go into a second marriage blindly for your own sake, as well as for the sake of your children. Howard and I talked through many scenarios, including what should happen if we die at the same time, what to do if either of us dies first, and then a different plan if one of us marries a third time. These complications usually don't cause concern entering into a first marriage, but I believe we must think it all through if we choose to remarry, especially if the marriage involves children or the accumulation of wealth.

Be Prepared

One can never fully prepare, but we should at least know ahead of time some of the obstacles to expect. Remarriage is a beautiful gift, but it comes with a surprising number of challenges. When we married the first time, we left father and mother and started fresh, as two young people usually owning pretty much nothing. In a second marriage, this setup changes quite dramatically.

In second marriages, both sides have likely accumulated lots of stuff—possibly money, furniture, real estate—as well as the children we had with our first spouse. What happens to these things requires conversations and plans.

In addition to possessions, when we remarry after the death of a spouse, grief tags along. We can't escape it. If we don't enter in knowingly, the dynamics resulting from grief can destroy our new marriage and us.

Blending

When we remarry, we blend families, furniture, decorations, recipes, traditions, and cultures. Believe me, these six items add up to a lot of emotion, particularly if our children are old enough to care about the details. These pieces stress any marriage, but when you add children to the mix, the depth of stress and trial multiply with each child. Our blended family has seven children total. Yes, seven. Though only five (all teenagers) lived full-time under our roof after Howard and I married. I described the joy, pain, and sheer mayhem of joining our two families in this excerpt from my blog entry: "The Thing about Holidays."

> Blessed to find unimaginable happiness in remarriage, we marveled at the difficulties which came with this choice. Blending families brought with it both joy and pain. Thankfulness that life didn't end when Brian and Ann died, and the realization that happiness *can* coexist with loss.
>
> Disappointment, however, over the difficulties of blending family cultures, traditions, furniture, and menus. Five teenagers under one roof still grieving over the death of a parent rebelled against anything change-related, especially parental input [from their new mom or dad].
>
> Even now, four years into this wonderful marriage, and down to only one teen at home, we often catch ourselves "knocked to the mat," as Howard states in his book, *Honest Wrestling*. Although it should no longer surprise us, grief continually attacks like a burglar in the night.
>
> We find happiness again. We learn to enjoy the "new normal." We appreciate the new gifts God gives us. But the love, life, and memories we shared with the dead don't just go away because they left this earth.

A counselor warned us to expect another round of grief once we married. Oh, boy! Turns out he knew all about our impending turmoil. Not only did we experience another round of grief just before engagement, but we also drew out another round after the wedding—at times one person at a time, and then everyone at once. Each expressed it in their own not-so-pretty way.

Some withdrew to their rooms. Others loudly commanded attention at the dinner table. Some picked fights over stupid stuff with the "safe" family-of-origin, while others complained in private to their DNA parent. Silent wars of "them vs. us" took over. Eating disorders ensued. Raging tempers flared.

Howard and I just wanted to enjoy our newlywed status! Almost every evening we dealt with at least one enormous teenage issue. Most evenings we fell into bed exhausted from the emotion of dealing with numerous emotionally stressed teenagers.

I really don't recommend getting married with five teenagers at home, but we did it and survived. Little by little, and with a ton of money spent on counseling, we made slow, steady progress.

According to Ron Deal, it takes about five to seven years to fully blend families, and "a strong marriage is critical for the relational development of the children."[5] We might just make it, while our counselor runs off to purchase a new boat with our money.

Reverse Grief

I experienced a new kind of grief, which I dubbed "reverse grief." I grieved the future I didn't get to enjoy with Brian, the past I missed out on with Howard, and the history we didn't get to develop with each other's children. This was *not* what I signed up for! Nevertheless we needed to work through it.

Howard and I prioritized date night, and with time, we created our own memories. Howard often reminded me, "See, Fran, we have history."

The teenage issues, however, stretched and challenged our marriage. Almost every argument revolved around the kids. I pleaded with Howard to treat the children more gently. He pleaded with me to not usurp his authority. More counseling.

We owe our marriage and our blending accomplishments to our wonderful Christian counselor, Rick. Some of the teens took turns in counseling, and I went every other week to talk through the skirmishes we experienced with each teenager, as well as how these disputes affected our marriage. Howard greatly trusted and respected the counselor. He listened intently to the advice I gleaned from my time with Rick, and we worked together to implement his advice.

At one point we visited one of Howard's best friends whose seven children came from one marriage. As we talked, we realized their teenage brawls sounded just like ours. Here we thought our problems surfaced because of blending families, but we realized teenagers are teenagers, whether we birth them or not. This gave us hope, a sense of normalcy, and a little bit of peace.

Pictures

You may disagree with me here, and that's okay, but I believe the word "blending" serves as the key word. When my daughter first read my communication with Howard, she immediately liked him. "Mom you gotta marry this guy. He won't make us take our pictures off the wall." When we blend families, we must also blend pictures, family heirlooms, and furniture, unless you choose to purchase all new furniture together.

Think about this for a minute. Pictures represent our memories. They depict our entire story. Why would we remarry, blend families, and not include pictures of our former lives? In addition to his mom, I actually owe Ann a thank you for helping to smooth out the rough edges in Howard. Whether I like it or not, a part of Ann comes with choosing Howard. I need to embrace that, and her, if I want him to embrace and accept Brian's influence in my life.

When you walk into our home, the main hallway tells our story. At the front of our house hang large pictures of our first families. Farther down the wall, our wedding picture with all seven children tells a different story. Throughout our home you will find pictures of the Joslins and pictures of the Geigers, as well as pictures of what we now dub the "Josgers."

We even hung a picture with three slots. On one side sits Howard and Ann's wedding picture. The other side holds Brian's and my wedding picture, and the middle one displays the wedding picture of Howard and me. We celebrate both families because we *are* both families.

If we take down all of the pictures, we basically tell our children their dead parent means nothing to us anymore. Keeping the pictures up doesn't mean we need to worship those pictures or place them on our bedroom wall. Howard moved into my house, which was difficult for him and his children. I removed my wedding pictures from my bedroom walls but kept pictures of Brian and me on the dresser. I also added pictures of Howard and Ann to the same dresser. Wedding pictures of Howard and me took the place of honor on our bedroom walls.

I recognize this is easier for couples where both are widowed. Char, a ninety-two-year-old widow lost her first husband at age twenty-three in World War II. They shared no children. When she remarried at age twenty-eight, she told her new husband she wanted to hang pictures with her first husband in their home. Widowed again after a second marriage of forty-some years, this time with children, she still proudly displays both husbands.

My point? Think twice before marrying again, if your new love can't include your family, your memories, and your pictures.

Jealousy

Have I ever been jealous of Ann? Yes, indeed. How do I manage it? I flip the story, and then think and act logically. I flip the story around by reminding myself of my desire to remember and love Brian. If I want the freedom to tell my stories and hold onto my love for Brian, I owe Howard the same courtesy. I must then think and act logically. Once I recognize my need to keep memories of Brian in my life, I can logically talk myself into managing my envy.

I must also think about my own love for Howard. My love for Brian doesn't change my love for Howard. My love for Brian, therefore, holds no threat to Howard and vice versa. Howard's love for Ann holds no threat to his love for me. Now I can manage my feelings.

Another little tidbit of information I will throw out there for free: We will like some things better about our dead spouse than we do our new one. We will also like some things better about our new spouse than we did our deceased one. This is simply a fact of life. It holds true with friendships, children, and extended family. Things crop up that we don't like, but other characteristics we adore.

My mom always said, "No man is perfect. You simply must find the one whose faults you can live with." I hope you can adore your new husband for his positive qualities and not dwell on the negatives. Jealousy will crop up, however, if you dwell on comparing your new spouse's negatives to your deceased spouse's positives. This causes trouble. Try to embrace both as totally different individuals who contain both wonderful qualities and not-so-wonderful ones.

The "S" Word

Let's be honest. Many widows feel they've been deprived of so many things, including sex, and if we decide to remarry, we eagerly anticipate expressing love to our new mate sexually.

May I remind you that grief follows us into our new marriages? What that means: grief, and your sexual memories from your first marriage will follow you into the marriage bed. No one expects to shut down on their wedding night, especially when they excitedly anticipate this day.

Consider yourself forewarned. Grief can suck the fun out of your wedding night, your honeymoon, and your marriage. Another step forward—remarriage. One step backward—memories and a new kind of grief. This new marriage, and now sex, with someone new, serves as another reminder of our loss. It can bring with it an unwelcomed flood of emotion and grief when you most want to forget your pain and enjoy your new relationship status.

I shut down emotionally on my first date with Howard, and we both shut down sexually on our honeymoon. Suddenly we stood bare before someone new, and raw emotion erupted. Another step toward each other reminded us that we would not enter into this new marriage without the losses that preceded it. Although we eagerly anticipated our new sexual freedom, what came naturally and felt familiar in our first marriages unexpectedly felt foreign with a new mate. Thankfully we could talk and pray about it, cry together, and work through it.

Don't jump into remarriage for sex. You might just find yourself extremely disappointed. With time and effort, couples can work through even sexual surprises. The best solution? Talk to each other about your feelings, pray and work together as a team, and seek counsel if necessary. Share your own needs and desires without blaming or accusing, and recognize this as part of the fallout from loss.

Should I Remarry?

After reading my story, you might not want anything to do with remarriage. I don't blame you. Especially the teenage part. Although extremely difficult, I think marriage is wonderful and well worth the effort. You must decide for yourself.

Howard and I are happier than we've been in years. No one in the house fights cancer. As the children mature and leave the nest, more and more peace settles on our home. We started a ministry and love working together. The first couple of years tested everything in us, but we made it through. We live united as one, and thank the Lord daily that we no longer face life alone.

I *now* agree with Jerry Sittser. "Life *can* still be good, just not the same way it was before,"[6] (emphasis mine).

> So they are no longer two, but one flesh. Therefore what God has joined together, let no one separate.
>
> Mathew 19:6, Mark 10:9

WE'RE GONNA MAKE IT, BABE!

When the doctor informed us our first child entered the world with a heart condition, Brian coined the phrase,

"We're gonna make it, Babe."

When our second son presented with severe asthma, Brian reminded me,

"We're gonna make it, Babe.

When our monthly medical expenses equaled half of our mortgage payment, Brian repeated it:

"We're gonna make it, Babe."

When his CT scan indicated an "impressive tumor," he held his stance.

"We're gonna make it, Babe."

As I drove my car after hearing Brian experienced a seizure while flying to Midland, Texas, I shook with fear. I prayed for strength and determined that—no matter what—I would make it.

I had no clue what lay ahead of us. Brain surgery for Brian, chemo-therapy, radiation, nine years of fighting for his life, only to lose the war, and the horrendous grief that followed. If I had known on October 14, 1999, what the next ten to fifteen years would look like for me, I might've given up. God blesses us by not revealing all the details up front.

As I near the completion of this book, I truly stand in awe. Sixteen years have flown by, and I am still making it. I survived. My children progressed from eight, five and barely two years old to twenty-four, twenty-one, and almost eighteen. Tears begin to flow as the magnitude of this achievement penetrates my heart.

Somewhere along the line we find a way to scratch our way out of the darkness of death. While we still grieve, we encounter more joy than sadness, and we discover how to keep living. I pray this book provides you with some maps for the road you travel, and that you will soon look back and discover you made it too.

When I married Howard and the kids rebelled, he adopted the phrase,

"We're gonna make it, Babe."

When I hesitantly agreed to take on the presidency of Howard's ministry vision, he reminded me,

"We're gonna make it, Babe."

When I feel insecure about my ability to write a book for widows, Howard tells me,

"You're gonna make it, Babe."

When all else fails, Howard asks me, "What would Brian say?" I always know the answer.

"We're gonna make it, Babe."

When you find yourself deep in the throes of grief, let me remind you,

"We're gonna make it, Babe."

ENDNOTES

Introduction

1. Widow's Hope, "These Are the Statistics" http://www.widowshope.org/first-steps/these-are-the-statistics/(accessed August 24, 2015).

Part One: When Death Strikes

1   Merriam-Webster's, http://www.merriam-webster.com/dictionary/shock (accessed August 24, 2015).

2   Kenneth C. Haugk, *A Time to Grieve* (St. Louis: Stephen Missions, 2004), 7.

3   Teresa TL Bruce, Teal Ashes, "What to Say When Someone Dies," http://tealashes.com/2013/11/18/you-shouldnt-say-you-should/ (accessed August 20, 2015).

4   WebMD "Grief and Grieving – Symptoms," http://www.webmd.com/balance/tc/grief-and-grieving-symptoms (accessed August 20, 2015).

5   Jerry Sittser, *A Grace Disguised* (Grand Rapids: Zondervan, 2004), 29.

6   Ibid., 43.

7   Kübler-Ross, Elisabeth & Kessler, David "The Five Stages of Grief," http://grief.com/the-five-stages-of-grief/ (accessed August 20, 2015).

8   Recover from Grief "7 Stages of Grief: Through the Process and Back to Life," http://www.recover-from-grief.com/7-stages-of-grief.html (accessed August 20, 2015).

9   Genden, Jojo, Live Strong "3 Stages of Grief," http://www.livestrong.com/article/111048-stages-grief/(accessed August 20, 2015).

10 Dana Barfield, *My Friend Just Lost Her Husband* (Plano: TBG, 2009), 39.

11 Sittser, *A Grace Disguised*, 61.

12 The Nebraska Department of Veterans' Affairs "What is PTSD (Posttraumatic Stress Disorder)?" http://www.ptsd.ne.gov/what-is-ptsd.html (accessed August 20, 2015).

13 Anxiety and Depression Association of America "PostTraumatic Stress Disorder," http://www.adaa.org/understanding-anxiety/posttraumatic-stress-disorder-ptsd (accessed August 20, 2015).

14   WebMd "Post-Traumatic Stress-Disorder – Treatment," http://www.webmd.com/mental-health/tc/post-traumatic-stress-disorder—treatment-overview (accessed August 20, 2015).

15   Sittser, *A Grace Disguised*, 73.

16   James Means, *A Tearful Celebration*, (Multnomah Publishers, Inc., 2006), 61.

17   Sittser, *A Grace Disguised*, 91.

18   Susan J. Zonnebelt-Smeenge & Robert C. DeVries, *Getting to the Other Side of Grief* (Grand Rapids: Baker, 2001), 140.

19   Haugk, *Experiencing Grief,* 7, 8.

20   Weitzman, Nancy "The Three Stages of Grief" http://www2.sunysuffolk.edu/pecorip/SCCCWEB/ETEXTS/DeathandDying_TEXT/Three-Stages-of-Grief.htm (accessed August 20, 2015).

21   David & Nancy Guthrie, *When Your Family's Lost a Loved One,* (Carol Stream: Tyndale House, 2008), 167.

22   Ibid., 167.

23   "One Day at a Time Sweet Jesus," Written by Marijohn Wilkin and Kris Kristofferson, 1974.

24   "Day by Day with Each Passing Moment," written by A. L. Skoog; Carolina Sandell, 1865.

Part Two: When Death Sucks the Life out of You

1   Merriam-Webster "Dictionary Entry – Loss," http://www.merriam-webster.com/dictionary/loss?show=0&t= 1363401623 (accessed August 20, 2015).

2   Sittser, *A Grace Disguised*, 72, 73.

3   Ibid., 82.

4   "Oh Stop the World and Let Me Off," written by Carl Belew, W. S. Stevenson, Four Star Records, Here's Patsy Cline, 1960.

5   American Academy of Sleep Medicine http://www.aasmnet.org (accessed August 20, 2015).

6   WebMd "Grief and Grieving – Symptoms," http://www.webmd.com/balance/tc/grief-and-grieving-symptoms (accessed August 20, 2015).

7   Doug Manning, *The Pain of Grief* (Oklahoma City: In-Sight Books, 2002), 19.

8   Merrill, Dixie, "On the Death of My Beloved," poem excerpt from "The New Normal" *Chera Fellowship newsletter*, http://ifcamedia.org/ifcaweb/pubs/ifcachera/CHERACURRENT.pdf. (accessed August 20, 2015).

9   *Honest Wrestling* by K. Howard Joslin is to be re-released as *Frayed* in 2015.

10 Leslie Vernick, *The Emotionally Destructive Relationship* (Eugene: Harvest House, 2005), 8.

11 As elsewhere in the book, italics represent my own emphasis.

12 Sittser, *A Grace Disguised*, 112.

13 Ibid., 116.

14 Ibid., 118.

15 Stephen Altrogge, The Blazing Center "Grace for Today, and Not a Drop More," http://theblazingcenter.com/2012/02/grace-for-today-and-not-a-drop-more.html (accessed August 20, 2015).

16 Ron L. Deal, *The Smart Stepfamily: Seven Steps to a Healthy Family* (Minneapolis: Bethany House, 2009) 68.

17 Eve Tahmincioglu, NBC News "Workers' Bereavement Benefits Often Fall Short," http://www.nbcnews.com/id/22823365/ns/business-careers/t/workers-bereavement-benefits-often-fall-short/#.VcVf2_lVikq (accessed August 20, 2015).

18 Eve Tahmincioglu, NBC News "Workers' Bereavement Benefits Often Fall Short," http://www.nbcnews.com/id/22823365/ns/business-careers/t/workers-bereavement-benefits-often-fall-short/#.VcVf2_lVikq (accessed August 20, 2015).

19 Gary Smalley, Simple Marriage, "Preparing Hearts for Remarriage" http://simplemarriage.net/preparing-hearts-for-remarriage/ (accessed August 19, 2015).

20 Georg McConnel, "Pornography and Virtual Infidelity," http://www.focusonthefamily.com/marriage/divorce_and_infidelity/pornography_and_virtual_infidelity/stages_of_porn_addiction.aspx (accessed August 20, 2015).

21 Your Brain on Porn, http://yourbrainonporn.com/tools-for-change (accessed August 19, 2015).

22 Merriam-Webster "Dictionary Entry for Adultery," http://www.merriam-webster.com/dictionary/adultery?show=0&t=1361832540 (accessed August 19, 2015).

23 Merriam-Webster.com, "Dictionary Entry for Fornication," http://www.merriam-webster.com/dictionary/fornication (accessed August 19, 2015).

24 WaitingTillMarriage.org, "Waiting Works: Couples Who Wait Report 22% Happier Marriages (and Better Sex!)" http://waitingtillmarriage.org/study-couples-who-waited-have-happier-more-stable-marriages/ (accessed August 19, 2015).

25 2014 State of Dating in America, by ChristianMingle.com http://www.stateofdatingreport.com/findings.htm (accessed August 19, 2015).

26 Christopher & Angela Yuan, *Out of a Far Country* (Colorado Springs: WaterBrook, 2011), 187-188.

27 Zonnebelt-Smeege & De Vries, *Getting to the Other Side of Grief*, 98.

28 Glen Stanton, "How We Dishonor God in Our Sex Lives." Focus on the Family, http://www.focusonthefamily.com/marriage/sex_and_intimacy/gods_design_for_sex/how_we_dishonor_god_in_our_sex_lives.aspx (accessed Aug. 19, 2015).

29 Matt Slick, Christian Apologetics and Research Ministry, "Is Masturbation Wrong?" https://carm.org/masturbation (accessed Aug. 19, 2015).

30 Guthrie, *When Your Family's Lost a Loved One*, 5.

31 Max Lucado, *Facing Your Giants* (Nashville: W Publishing, 2006), 84.

32 Zonnebelt-Smeede & DeVries, *Getting to the Other Side of Grief*, 69.

33 K. Howard Joslin, *Honest Wrestling* (Plano: Authenticity Book House, 2012), 198.

34 Ibid., 198.

Part Three: When Death No Longer Wins

1 Means, A Tearful Celebration, 130.

2 Gary Smalley, Simple Marriage, "Preparing Hearts for Remarriage" http://simplemarriage.net/preparing-hearts- for-remarriage/ (accessed August 19, 2015).

3 Deal, *The Smart Stepfamily: Seven Steps to a Healthy Family*, 11.

4 Ibid., 76.

5 Ibid., 26.

6 Sittser, *A Grace Disguised*, 91.

HELPFUL RESOURCES

http://simplemarriage.net/preparing-hearts-for-remarriage/

www.griefshare.org –GriefShare has many resources for all kinds of grief, including divorce recovery, single parenting, sexual purity, etc.

A Grace Disguised by Jerry Sittser

Honest Wrestling (to be re-released as *Frayed* in 2015) by K. Howard Joslin

https://anewseason.net/category/widows-might/

Reflections of a Grieving Spouse by H. Norman Wright

A Tearful Celebration by James Means

When Your Family's Lost a Loved One by David and Nancy Guthrie

Let Me Grieve, but not Forever by Verdell Davis

Hope and Help for the Widow by Jan Sheble

BIBLIOGRAPHY

Barfield, Dana. *My Friend Just Lost Her Husband* (Plano: TBG, 2009), 39.

Deal, Ron L. *The Smart Step Family: Seven Steps to a Healthy Family.* Minneapolis: Bethany House, 2006.

Guthrie, David & Nancy. *When Your Family's Lost a Loved One.* Carol Stream: Tyndale House, 2008.

Haugk, Kenneth C. *Experiencing Grief.* St. Louis: Stephen Missions, 2004.

Joslin, K. Howard, *Honest Wrestling* (Plano: Authenticity Book House, 2012; to be re-released as Frayed in 2015).

Haugk, Kenneth C. *A Time to Grieve.* St. Louis: Stephen Missions, 2004.

Haugk, Kenneth C. *Finding Hope and Healing.* St. Louis: Stephen Missions, 2004.

Lewis, C. S. *The Complete C. S. Lewis Signature Classics* (New York Harper Collins, 2002)

Lucado, Max. *Facing Your Giants.* Nashville: W Publishing, 2006.

Manning, Doug. *The Pain of Grief.* Oklahoma City: In-Sight Books, 2002.

Means, James. *A Tearful Celebration.* Sisters: Multnomah, 2006.

Rabey, Lois Mowday. *When Your Soul Aches.* Colorado Springs: WaterBrook, 2004.

Sheble, Jan. *Hope & Help for the Widow: The Reality of Being Alone.* Chattanooga: AMG, 2003.

Sittser, Jerry. *A Grace Disguised* (Grand Rapids: Zondervan, 2004), 29.

Vernick, Leslie. *The Emotionally Destructive Relationship.* Eugene: Harvest House, 2005.

Wright, H. Norman. *Reflections of a Grieving Spouse*. Eugene: Harvest House, 2009.

Yuan, Christopher & Angela. *Out of a Far Country*. Colorado Springs: WaterBrook, 2011.

Zonnebelt-Smeenge, Susan J. & De Vries, Robert C. *Getting to the Other Side of Grief*. Grand Rapids: Baker, 2001.

ABOUT THE AUTHOR

Fran Geiger Joslin was born to missionary parents in the jungles of Indonesia. She married Brian Geiger in 1989. Ten years later their world came crashing down as her husband received a terminal cancer diagnosis.

Brian lost his battle with the disease almost nine years later. Devastated by the loss of her best friend, Fran, along with her kids, clung to the Lord to pick up the pieces in their shattered lives.

By God's amazing grace, just two and one half years after Brian's death, Fran met and married a widower named Howard Joslin, combining a total of seven children, five of whom were teenagers when they married.

Fran enjoys writing and mentoring young women. She serves as President of Authenticity Book House, a non-profit publishing ministry, which she and Howard started together in 2014. They aim to change the paradigm of traditional publishing to ministry as the bottom line.

Connect with Fran:

FranGeigerJoslin.Wordpress.com

FranGeigerJoslin@gmail.com

www.Facebook.com/FranGeigerJoslin

@FranGJoslin

FranGeigerJoslin

The Ministry of ABH

Authenticity Book House is a nonprofit publishing ministry that:

- Serves gifted Christian authors by removing publishing barriers.
- Equips non-English speaking pastors and teachers with biblical literature in their heart languages.
- Employs skilled believers in developing nations.

Serving Aspiring Authors

- Authors own all copyrights.
- ABH absorbs all costs for cover design, editing, formatting, proofreading, translating, and marketing of the author's first three books.
- ABH does not take any royalties on sales of the author's first three books.

Equipping Pastors Worldwide

- 20 percent of net royalties on all ABH books goes to support international pastors.
- ABH targets strategic language groups that lack biblical resources.

Empowering Believers

- ABH selects authors with confirmed Christlike character and ministry effectiveness.
- ABH employs translators and editors around the globe.

Please help us glorify Christ in editorial excellence. If you find a mistake in this book, please e-mail the error and the page number to quality@abhbooks.com.